BROKEN SPIRIT
LET IT GO SO YOU CAN GROW

MARYAM BEY

To order additional copies of this book, contact:
Proisle Publishing Services LLC
1177 6th Ave 5th Floor
New York, NY 10036, USA
Phone: (+1 347-922-3779)
info@proislepublishing.com

PROISLE PUBLISHING

CONTENTS

DEDICATION

Dedications to Mary Ward Frazier Barnes, my mother. She was my best friend, and I loved her so much, until that dreadful day. My struggles and challenges in life began for me at fifteen years of age. I now realize my mother gave me what she had; she did her best and I'm not mad anymore. Due to my life challenges, I understand what happened to me was not my mother's fault. I blamed her as she blamed me, because we were both "broken spirits." When I was raped by my father, the bond we had until that day was stolen from us. I miss and love my mommy and I forgive her, may she Rest in Peace. Thank you to the sister at Pathmark in South Orange, NJ, for giving me the idea of writing *"Broken Spirit,"* and to Donna P., my friend, for reminding me to journal my experiences. Thank you, Bessie Walker, former Councilwoman At-Large Newark, NJ, Ms. Kotb, Director of Kintock, I knew Ms. Kotb for one year. However, prior to her leaving Kintock, she inspired me so much. Thank you, Ms. Gannon, Director of the Clinical Department at Delaney Hall. I thank these three amazing women who were not intimidated by my drive and desire to do what I loved—which was to teach. These women allowed me to apply my skills and experiences to create an environment that contributed toward the advancement of men and women who were reaching out for help. As a team, we successfully helped men and women overcome their life's challenges. Finally, thank you to the incredible brothers and sisters who were inmates at The Kintock Group, Delaney Hall, Logan Hall, Essex County Correctional Facility, from 2006 to 20016, and Newark Reentry. You taught me so much about human behavior that no book could teach me. I am successful in reentry because of you. Counselling and training you to help find your purpose directed me to discover mine. My interactions with you provided me the opportunity to acquire specific techniques by listening to your stories and sharing

i

your pain, your joy, and your challenges. To our children who attend public schools, you are our future, we are moving forward to ensure a quality education and social justice, so you do not become a "broken spirit." To counselors and teachers, you are so special; you are the magicians who can create a healthy wholistic environment for inmates, residents, and our students that will aid in the development of an unfolding future for these individuals, help expand of their horizons, and help them recognize their unlimited possibilities because you believe in them. Give your best. May God Bless You. To Curtis Jackson aka *50 Cent*. I listened to your music as I wrote *Broken Spirit: Let It Go So You Can Grow*. I completed the initial version of *Broken Spirit* in 2011; I had no idea that three years later I would meet *50*. On June 3, 2014, I met him at DTLR Sports Store in Livingston, NJ, with compliments of my campaign manager. He knew I liked *50*. I informed my Director I was leaving for the day. This was a window of opportunity I was not going to miss. I drove home to get *The 50th Law*, a book written collaboratively with Robert Greene. I wanted *50* to sign my copy of his book. The entrance fee was $15.00 to purchase Animal Ambition, 50's new CD. When they called me, *50* had such a big smile on his face. I said hi and took out the book I had hidden under my jacket. He said, "That's my book." I said "Yes, I want you to sign it." I told him I lectured on his book and on him at Delaney Hall. He smiled and said, "You did"? Yes, I did. We both smiled. At that time security was rushing me to go, but *50* said, "Hold it" to the guard. "What's your name?" he asked. I said "Ms. Bey." He said "Okay. I'm signing to Bey, Stay Sweet and God Bless. *50 Cent*." He asked me if I wanted him to sign his CD. I said sure. My goal is to interview *50* on my TV show "Tell a Vision" (www.tellavisiontav.com). You can see an announcement at the end of the Conclusion section at the back of this book. Writing this book has helped me realize that you do not have to be incarcerated to be a broken spirit. We have all been broken spirits at some time in our lives, no matter our age. Our challenges are a test. Once we pass the test, we become a testimony. I love Bishop TD Jakes' motto: **They want my glory not my story**, which means that people don't want to go through hard times and disappointments. The "Glory" is the reward; the "Story" is the work you put in. This book is dedicated to all the **Broken Spirits** who **Let It Go So They Could Grow**.

BROKEN SPIRIT:
LET IT GO SO YOU CAN GROW

Writing the revisions of Broken Spirit Let It Go So You Can Grow during Covid19 and the ongoing killing of Black and Brown people, I realized I was writing about those who had been broken by family members or those they knew in the first publication of Broken Spirit. Revising Broken Spirit Let It Go So You Can Grow, I recognized they/we had been broken by a society that creates human beings who are broken, unhappy, mentally unstable, and spiritually unbalanced and those who injure others have a sense of entitlement by preying on the weak.

In the original Broken Spirit Let It Go So You Can Grow, I introduced you to Tony Olajuwon in the chapter, The Coach. I also introduced you to Chris Stokes in the chapter, a Life Reclaimed – The Transformation. These gentlemen were on my caseload. Both used and applied their skills to live their purpose.

In the revision of Broken Spirit Let It Go So You Can Grow I introduce you to two enterprising gentlemen. Faheem Shabazz, CEO, Family Investors Real Estate Management and Lance McGraw, CEO, Lyrical Chef and HUSTLELUTION. I am sure you will be inspired by them as I have been. I highlight the abusive treatment of women in The Edna Mahan Prison for Women in New Jersey.

CLIENT WHO NEVER WORKED

The first time I heard of a person who never worked in their life was in 2003, when an inmate had been released from prison was required to work in order to stay out of prison was referred to me by another inmate. He asked me to help his friend get employment. This gentleman was fifty years old. I called him to make an appointment. The next day he came to my office bright and early, dressed in a green prison outfit. I asked him to have a seat. He apologized for being dressed in prison clothing, saying that he did not have any clothes since

1

being released from prison. He seemed embarrassed. His statement allowed me to begin our interview. I said to him, "You must be reading my mind." He smiled. I took out a pad to take notes. I admitted to him I did not know how to respond to the fact that a fifty-year-old man had never worked. I mentioned to him I was very curious how he took care of himself without working. His response was he "hustled." He appeared to be nervous and a little jittery. I asked him why he was uncomfortable. He said if he did not find a job, he would be sent back to prison. He had been in prison five years. I mentioned to him this was the first time I did not have any answers regarding helping someone who had never worked.

"So, when you say you hustled, do you mean you sold drugs?"

"Yes," was his response. He also said he robbed, boosted ... you know things along that line.

"So therefore, you do have skills that are transferrable."

"What do you mean?" was his reply.

I said, "When you sold drugs, you were a businessman, though it was illegal. You conducted an analysis of the corner or block you wanted to control, you observed to see if it was busy enough for you to make money, and if it was, you began selling your product which allowed you to pay your staff. So, you were a businessman. You were operating a business, which meant you have skills. You hired people to sell your drugs. You interviewed people, you managed them. You provided a location, work schedule, hours of work, and you marketed your product. You purchased and invested in your drugs. Your experiences have to be transferred into a resume."

He asked how he would do that.

I said, "You won't, I will."

He smiled. I referred him to Dress for Success which is an organization that provides clothing for interview. I asked him to return the next day to pick up his resume. I contacted a local agency in East Orange, NJ. I knew someone there and informed her about this brother and the fact that he had never worked. I apprised her of his history and spoke of his character. She asked if he could come in two days for an interview. I said yes. I called him to give him the information about the job and the location of Dress for Success, the name of the person he would be interviewing with, and the time and location of interview. I asked him to return to my office after the interview. He did everything I asked him to do. He came to my office after the interview, dressed in a suit, nice shoes, and hair done. He said to me, smiling, "Ms. Bey, I got the job. Thank you. You didn't know me, but you took a chance on me even though you knew what I had been doing all my life, thank-you. Why did you do that Ms. Bey?" I said to him, "Well, first congratulations on your job and I am so happy for you." "Secondly it is not for me to judge you. But since you asked, it was your attitude that impressed me. You were very respectful, you seemed serious, and it was obvious you wanted to work. I did what I was supposed to do to help a brother out."

He smiled, said thank-you, and walked out the office. I reminded him to let me know how he's doing from time to time. Two weeks passed, and the third week I received a call from the police officer who sat at the front desk informing me there was someone who wanted to speak to me. The officer told me who it was, I wondered why he came to the office rather than call me. I started thinking, "I hope he's not in trouble or had done something foolish." The closer I got to the front; I could see him. He too saw me, and stood up, holding a dozen roses. "Wow" I said, "Those are beautiful."

"These are for you, Ms. Bey."

"For what?" I said.

He said for finding me this job. I could not accept them, but I appreciated the thought. I asked him if he had a girlfriend. He said yes. I asked him to give the roses to her, and that I wouldn't reveal to her that these flowers were meant for me. Everyone started laughing. I had no idea this experience would help me in the future. I called Councilwoman Walker to let her know we got another brother hired.

EMPLOYMENT COUNSELOR/CASE MANAGER AT KINTOCK HALFWAY HOUSE

When Councilwoman Walker lost her position in May 2006, I started sending my resume to all positions requiring degrees. I remembered my college years and the sacrifices I made to obtain my degrees. At this moment it proved to be worth it, because were it not for my degrees and my experiences, I would not have been hired as an Employment Counselor at Kintock in October 2006. In June, a representative from Kintock called me for an interview. Of course, I said yes. I was so excited. I bought a new suit, a new briefcase, and nice shoes. The day I went to Kintock for the interview, I passed through metal detectors and was brought to a conference room with six people. I said "Whoa!" The Director asked if everything was alright. I said yes, and that I had not been aware I would be interviewed by a team.

"Do you have a problem with that?" she asked.

"No," I replied.

I breezed through their questions. The question of salary came up. I informed them what I was earning. The Director said that they could not match that. I said this was no problem and that I would accept the position because I believed this would be the best career decision I make. I was hired as an Employment Counselor. My responsibilities were to conduct pre-employment classes which prepared inmates with interview skills, dressing for success, responsibility, job skills, and of course job placement. This class was mandatory because for residents to go home, they had to be employed. It was also my responsibility to meet with company representatives and visit work sites. The first day I conducted the employment class, there were forty-five residents, both male and female. They were new and so was I. I introduced myself to them and asked how many had job? A few raised their hands. Others had been in prison for a while and had not worked in society for a number of years. One young man raised his hand and said, "Ms. Bey, I never worked."

His statement took me back to the 50-year-old inmate I had worked with when I was a Council Aide. "Okay," I said, "thank-you. You are how old?" I asked.

"Twenty-eight, Ms. Bey."

"How have you taken care of yourself all these years?" I asked him.

"I hustled," he said.

"By hustling," I asked him, "do you mean you sold drugs?"

His response was yes.

"So, you supported your family fifteen years by selling drugs?"

He responded yes. At that moment I was grateful for my experience with the fifty-year-old inmate, because otherwise I would have been shocked at the fact that this young man never worked at a legal job? I asked him if he realized what he was doing. He said he did not understand the question.

"Did you realize what you were doing when you were selling illegal drugs in our community?" I remarked. His response was typical.

"I was selling drugs to take care of my family. I was trying to find a job Ms. Bey, but what they were paying did not take care of my needs. I did not think I would get caught so I got caught up in the life, you know, fast money, women, cars, and one thing led to another. I was doing fine for a while. Look how long I been doing it he said."

"Yeah," I responded, "and look at where you are sitting saying it."

"You're right," he said. "What else could I do Ms. Bey?"

I asked him if he felt it was worth it. He said it was worth it at the time because he was helping his family. But that it was not worth it because he was sent to jail for more than three years. He was away from his family who he missed, and, while in prison, he had lost his grandmother. It hurt him that he was not home. As he was describing the part of regretting not being home when his grandmother died, tears welled up in his eyes. I asked if he was okay. He said yes. While I was asking these questions, other inmates were listening. I asked if he had his high school diploma. He said they put him out of school in the tenth grade.

"Oh, you dropped out?" I said.

"No, Ms. Bey, they put me out because I was fighting and getting in trouble."

"No, you dropped out." I responded.

"No, Ms. Bey, I was thrown out."

"Well," I stated, "you had the opportunity to go back to school, right?"

"Yes," he said.

"So, you chose not to. Though the principal put you out because of your behavior, you could have gone back to get your diploma. Therefore, you dropped out."

I explained to the class that what he did was typical of what many of us do. Make excuses or blame someone else for our problems rather than taking responsibility for our actions. I explained that what he had done was use being put out of school as an excuse to not go back to school. It was easy for him to justify or blame the system, and therefore, he would not have to take the responsibility of holding himself accountable for his behavior.

"Oh, I see what you are saying, Ms. Bey." he said.

I then asked the group if they understood what I was saying. They agreed, they also recognized themselves in that scenario. I mentioned to them that by accepting this belief, his attitude was: *They put me out, so I'm not going back, fuck them.*

"This was basically what he was saying right?"

"Yes," they replied, and so did he.

I asked him who did he hurt, the system or himself? He said, himself.

"So, what are you going to do about it?" I asked.

"I am going back and getting my GED," he replied.

"Why are you going back to get your GED? Is it because I am proposing that you go back or is it because it is something you really want to do?"

"Ms. Bey I really want to change my life, I am sick of this life, it isn't working, look at what it has done to me, look at where I am, I don't want to keep doing this."

"Well, that is why I am here," I said to him. "We will put a plan together and let's see what happens."

He smiled. I realized at that moment, is what I realized when I owned and operated Creative Garden School from 1975 to 1985 (my private school). One person *can* make a difference, and I made difference with this young man by having a discussion with him regarding changing his life from negative to positive. This is what I and my staff did with students at Creative Garden School, which was we inspired them to be success-driven, to believe in themselves, and to remind them that a mistake only makes them a better, more informed, and prepared human beings. I could do the same thing with these brothers and sisters. The reason why inmates and residents responded to me in such a positive way is because they knew I wanted them to be successful individuals for their children, their families, their communities and more importantly, themselves. They had to find an alternative to stop selling drugs and destroying their neighborhoods and their own lives.

7

This was one of those moments for me that I knew I was doing the right thing. I recognized that these brothers and sisters were the very students that the school system had failed. Their image of themselves had been destroyed and they were now "damaged goods." Why? Because many staff did not believe in them, they were pushed aside and through the system. They made bad decisions, and there was no one to advise them. I would now be their advisor.

I soon realized the men and women on my caseload were broken because of abuses they experienced as a child or adult, by family members, those they knew, and the society they lived in. When abuse happens as a child the child blames themselves, they think it was their fault. They grow up a broken adult if they do not address their unresolved past issues. If they do not heal their trauma it will continue to visit them. You cannot heal what you do not reveal. Think of some of the reasons you are broken and what needs to be revealed to heal.

Frederick Douglass, born into slavery February 14, 1818, supposedly stated, "it's easier to build strong children than to repair broken people". While some are researching if Frederick Douglas is the source of this quote, it makes sense to me. Why? He was a slave who escaped from slavery, became an Abolitionist, author, and freedom fighter in the 18th Century. So, I am confident he knew a thing or two about brokenness. The closet quotation they could find was in Frederick Douglass book "My Bondage and My Freedom". He states, "Once thoroughly broken down, who is he that can repair the damage?". Yes, the women and men on my caseload were damaged goods, I was damaged too. As I mentioned in this chapter, I would be their advisor, it was because I wanted them to recognize their internal issues so they can discover their greatness within.

Therefore, mental health care is so crucial to healing and why as a counselor I focused on behavioral issues rather than criminalize their behavior. As I was helping them to heal, I was healing too.

GANG MEMBER'S RISE TO THE TOP (J)

I want to tell you of a young man, I will call him J (not his real name). J was a 25-year-old young man who was transferred to the halfway house from Northern State Prison in Newark, NJ. He was typical in his style. His hair was in locks and wore baggy pants. He looked like the average drug dealer in our communities. J was always respectful toward me. He was on my caseload. As his Employment Counselor, it was my responsibility to find him a job. J did not have a high school diploma, like many of our young people in jail or prison. However, he was extremely talented, and like many of our young people who dropped out of school, he sold drugs and became involved in criminal activity. Once J completed his Employment Class, I found a job for him. I always give the guys and ladies a talk about my expectations of them when they are hired, you know, the dos and don'ts. For example, if they violate any condition of the Kintock Agreement, they could be sent back to prison. J went to the job assignment which was located at a temporary agency in the next town, Elizabeth, NJ. J called me to let me know there were no jobs at the time. He asked me for permission to go next door to get something to eat at the diner. I called the agency to confirm there were no jobs at the time. J called back, I gave him permission to go to the diner until the agency called back, I emphasized to him not go anywhere else. It was important for him to contact me because if not, he could be the subject of deviation, which would be a violation of his contract that could send him back to prison. However, a Kintock representative called to confirm if J was at the job site, the supervisor could not confirm because J did not tell his supervisor he was next door at the diner. You may ask why this was such a big deal. I too thought this way when I was first hired. The reality is that these men and women are the property of the State, it is the job of their counselors and agency to know where they are always located, because most crimes are committed while they claim they are working. There was a case a family was killed by inmates who lived at the halfway house. The inmates simply signed out to go to work and went to the next city to kill this family. Counselors must be careful and watchful of inmates when they are working or attending school. We must be careful since some inmates do deviate. They take these chances because they feel they will not get caught. Most times they don't. Anyway, back to J. When Administration learned J was at the diner, it was immediately reported to the Director. J lost his job, his visits, and was given a forty-five-day sanction. I felt the punishment was harsh usually the contract is 30 days. I was in my office, there was a knock on my office door. It was J, I asked him to come in. He was obviously angry, and of course I asked him what was wrong. I knew, but I wanted him to tell me in his own words.

"Ms. Bey this is not fair, I can't do this Ms. Bey."

He kept shaking his head, "No, no."

I asked him to just sit down and calm down. I asked him to tell me the problem.

"Ms. Bey they are sanctioning me to a forty-five-day contract. They are not supposed to do that, and Ms. Bey I can't do this contract, I'm going to have to leave."

"What do you mean leave?" I asked.

"I'm going to have to break out."

I told him to think about his decision.

"Well what else can I do Ms. Bey?"

"First, you cannot escape," I said. "Second, why do you think you were given a forty-five-day contract?"

"Because Ms. Bey, I am affiliated."

"Affiliated?" I said. I just assumed he was speaking of being a member of a fraternity or something. At this point in my career, I was not yet informed or educated about gangs, what to look for, etc. That is why I asked him, what fraternity? You are not attending college so how are you affiliated? He started laughing. I asked him what was so funny.

"I'm in a gang, Ms. Bey."

"A gang?" I said.

Then we both started laughing. He realized I did not know. He had assumed I was told he was a gang member with status. I told him I would speak to the Director to let him know I gave J permission to go to the diner, and that I would get back to him. I was called to the Director's office. The director wanted to know if I knew where J was. I said yes, I gave him permission to go next door to the diner once I confirmed with the agency he was waiting for a job. The director also asked if I knew J was a high-ranking gang member, I said no, J never mentioned that to me. The director asked me why I did not ask J if he was a gang member. My response was if I asked that question, I am assuming all inmates were in a gang and I did not believe that. I let the director know I disagreed with the sanction and I went back to my office. I asked J to come to my office. I confirmed he was getting forty-five days and that I let the director know I disagreed with the sanction.

"It is what it is J, and after learning all this about you, I'm going to give you this advice. You said you want to leave right?" He said yes.

"I'm not a gang member but what I know is this, you won't get credit or recognition by your crew if you walk out of a halfway house. If you broke out of Northern State Prison that's different. Up until now you have done everything, I asked of you. I have not had any problems with you. So, this is what I am asking you to do. Don't walk out the door, please. It will not do anything for your credibility. I need you to promise me that when I come back to work tomorrow, you will be here. I will worry about you all night. Furthermore, I want you to think about what you will be doing to your grandmother and family. You just came home from prison. If you do decide to walk out that door, you know that will be another charge. You just started seeing your family. Why would you do that to them?"

"I just can't do it, Ms. Bey. Forty-five days!"

I said, "I know and agree it is harsh. But I am looking at it another way."

"What do you mean Ms. Bey?"

"I don't like the punishment," I repeated to him. "Sometimes we are tested for various reasons. Now you said you were going to run, right?"

"Yes."

"Don't you think that when this contract was given to you, they thought that as well? They were hoping you would do just what you said, run. They know if you do that, they get you a few more years. Now, you are an intelligent young man, they see that as well. You have status in your gang, which I don't particular care for. You're a leader, I have said that to you not knowing you were in a gang, I saw those skills just as they did. Why don't you do the unexpected that would shock them?"

"I don't think I can do it Ms. Bey."

"Yes, you can if you follow my advice. I promise when this is over, when you come through this and you will, you will thank me. So, if you want to cry, go ahead, but please don't try to escape, please don't do that and don't take this out on anyone because you are angry. Do what they ask, and I am telling you, you will see just how great you are."

I told him I can't hug him, but the day he is released, I would give him a big hug. He smiled.

"I'm praying I will see you tomorrow. I mentioned to him I would bring something for him to read that would help him get through this.

"And listen, I am giving you the same advice I would give my son if he were in your position," I said.

As he walked out the door, his head was down, he looked broken, his face was tight, and I prayed he would not run. I left the office late that night as I always do. J was on my mind. That night I did not sleep well because I was worried about J. I woke up at 6 a.m., got dressed and went to work. The first thing I did when I got to work was go to the abscond journal to see if J's name was in it. It wasn't, I was so relieved. As I went to my office, one of the inmates said, "Good morning Ms. Bey, you are here early."

"Yeah," I responded, "I have to see someone early this morning."

"Can I help you with your bags, Ms. Bey?"

"Yes, thank you." I said.

I got into my office and called J over the speaker to report to my office. A few minutes later, there was a knock on my door, it was J. I was so glad to see him. I smiled.

"Good morning Ms. Bey," he said, in kind of a beaten voice.

"Good morning, you know I am so glad to see you, I did not sleep worrying about you."

"I'm sorry Ms. Bey."

"Oh no, that was not your fault, it was my choice. Have a seat. So how do you feel?"

"Angry," he replied.

"That is a natural reaction," I said. "So why did you decide not to escape?"

13

"Well, I thought about what you said. I don't want to get another charge and I just started seeing my family after many years and it feels good to see them. I don't want to put them through this anymore."

"I am so glad you did some thinking. I like that," I said. "You thought about your family rather than yourself."

He nodded.

"I'm proud of you," I said. "Now I want you to read this."

I gave him an article that was done by one of my favorite ministers. I asked him to read it, write his thoughts and come back to see me the next day.

"Okay, Ms. Bey."

As he walked out the door, I said, "Keep your **HEAD UP**." He smiled. I asked him to come to my office every day, because each day I would have something for him to read, and if he wanted to talk to me, all he had to do was submit a request slip and I would see him ASAP. Each morning, J would make it his business to stop by and say good morning. Each day his face would get lighter. Not the type of light that refers to skin color, but the kind that is associated with "I got this" or "I am going to make it." That's what I am talking about. He had that "they are not going to destroy me" confidence. Each morning we had our special smile; we knew what was going on. In the beginning they thought J was going to escape or do something stupid. I believe they wanted him to do that. When it did not happen, the staff were bewildered because under normal circumstances J would have escaped. That was J's first response, and had I not been there as his counselor, he would have walked out. He said I encouraged him and helped him to see another way instead of the old way. The old way included wrong choices, the old way got him in trouble, and even though he was a gang member, the reality was he was a "broken spirit." I recognized that and wanted to uplift this young man. My talking to him each day made his day.

Particularly mine, because I knew each day J was in the facility, he was getting a day closer to the realization that he would become a testimony for somebody. He made me feel proud. As we got closer to J's final days of sanction, he came to my office one day, excited. He did not knock on my door.

"Excuse me, J, I did not give you permission to enter my office. Is there a problem?" I asked him.

"No, Ms. Bey. I apologize, let me do this the right way," he said.

He went out the office and knocked on the door. I smiled and motioned him to come in.

"So, what's up J?"

"Ms. Bey," he said with enthusiasm, "I did my first lecture today."

"What, and you didn't tell me?!"

He was grinning from cheek to cheek. There was so much pride in his face. His eyes were glistening, and he seemed so happy. I was happy to see this young man, who, just a month ago, was a "broken spirit." I was so proud of him. You know when you are working in a position you love even though it is not paying you the money you deserve, but you love what you do? It is times like these that make it all worthwhile for counselors who are questioning if they are doing the right thing. When you see a "J" realize their potential, you know therefore you are here currently at this moment for a reason. As J was talking to me and telling me his experience in his journey, I beamed with pride. J was telling me this standing up. I was sitting down and looking up at him, just smiling. I had known he would be successful in this test, I just had to get him to believe in himself.

"Ms. Bey," his voice cracked. "Ms. Bey, I just want to thank you for believing in me. You are the first person who ever believed in me, Ms. Bey. You are like my mother, Ms. Bey."

Tears rolled down his eyes. I got up from my desk to close the blinds on the door; I did not want anyone seeing him crying; this was a breakthrough moment for him. He was releasing his pain; I wanted no interruptions.

"Ms. Bey, I didn't believe in me, Ms. Bey," he said. "Thank-you, Ms. Bey, we made it."

"Well, I knew you would as long as you allowed me to do what I said I would do, you did, and these are the results. J, I saw your potential, the blessing is that you were open to listen to me."

"I love you, Ms. Bey."

"I love you too J," I said, "and I am proud of you."

I gave him some tissues to wipe his tears away. He said, "Ms. Bey, how is your son?"

"My son?" I said curiously. I didn't expect that.

"Yeah, you said he had been arrested."

"Oh."

I shook my head up and down, right, right. I had completely forgotten I told him about my son and his arrest. I said he was fine.

"It's placing an emotional toll on us, but he is going to be alright."

"I am praying every day for him," J said.

I thanked him.

"Because you know, unlike you, he has never been in jail. Like you, both of you are the same age. Like you, he is smart, he is a leader, and he has potential, just like you."

"This is something I hate."

"Yeah, J it is taking its toll on me. I am fighting to keep my son out of this system. You know what helps me to deal with this and my son's arrest?"

"What Ms. Bey?" he said.

"It is helping young brothers and sisters like you. It reminds me what my purpose is. I look forward to coming to work. To seeing your face and knowing that you are finding yourself and that makes me proud. My son is going to be alright. It's how we get out of this that concerns me. But thank you so much for asking me about him."

"Ms. Bey, it's going to be alright," he said.

"Thank you, J. I probably shared his situation with you because I wanted you to know that everybody is going through something. Doesn't matter how old they are, what color they are, what financial status they are, how rich, how poor they are. Everybody is going through something. How we go through it, determines how we come through it."

"What you mean Ms. Bey?"

"Well, we can go through our experiences and come out bitter and angry, hurtful, spiteful, wanting revenge, being violent and so on or we grow through it. Meaning, get the lesson out of it."

"I don't understand Ms. Bey, what exactly do you mean?"

"This is what I mean J. I am not going to let this challenge break me or my son. It's hard. I don't know the outcome. What I do know is that when we come out of this, we will know more than we did before this crisis. I will be able to help someone who may go through the same thing I went through. Like what you went through. You are now a testimony of success and you will tell your story. Give them advice based on your own personal experience. Congratulations." He smiled.

MY YOUNGEST SON'S ARREST

I can remember it like it was yesterday. It was June, a nice warm night, about 11:00 p.m. I was preparing to get off work; I worked a double as I normally do on Saturday to make extra money. I called to check my messages on my answering machine. The first message I heard was from my neighbor saying, "Maryam, T was arrested in Union." My heart stopped. I got nervous. At one point I could not speak. I got my composure and called the Union Township Police Department.

"Hell-o," I said, "this is Ms. Bey, I understand my son has been arrested and I am trying find out why he was arrested. Is he alright, I mean you guys did not do anything to my son, did you?" The operator asked me to calm down and she gave the direct number to call. I called the police department and identified myself. I spoke to a lieutenant. He explained to me that my son had been arrested because he was carrying a gun—two as a matter of fact. I asked what the problem was since he had his permit to carry and all his identification, so I didn't understand.

"You guys haven't done anything to my son, have you? He has not been harmed by you, has he?"

"No, no," the officer responded, "he is fine."

"Okay, give me the directions to get there." He gave me the directions, but I knew it would be difficult for me to get to the police department because I was too nervous. My son had never been arrested. He worked in a correctional facility as a corrections officer and that is as far as it went, he had never been inside a jail cell. I called my neighbor who called me about my son being arrested to ask him if he knew where the police station was in Union and if he could take me there. He asked me if I was at work? I told him I was just getting off work at Kintock. He told me he would be right there. I did not mention in the first publication that my neighbor who called me about my youngest son's arrest was due to my next door neighbor calling him to let me know since they did not have my phone number. Waiting for him to arrive felt like an eternity; I was so nervous. I called my youngest daughter to let her know what happened and talking to her while I was waiting for my friend to arrive kind of calmed my nerves. My neighbor eventually drove up and I got into the truck. We were there in fifteen minutes. We went into the police department, and I identified myself. I asked them again if my son was alright and if he had any bruises on him, they kept saying no and that he was fine. "Can you let him know I am here?"

The officer said, "Yes, he is pretty upset", I guess so I replied.

"I would be too if you arrested me for carrying my legal guns."

He went to my son to let him know I was in the police department.

"The officer came back and said your son wants to be sure it's you, so give me something that will let him know it is you." "I said tell him that "Omie" is outside."

Omie is the Islamic word for mother. He does not call me that, my older children do. However, I knew he would know it was me if I asked the officer to tell him that. The officer went to see him and came back out shortly and said he was fine. I was relieved. I asked if I could speak with him, and the officer said I could not. I then asked, "How much is his bail?"

The officer said, "one hundred thousand dollars."

I repeated, "a hundred thousand dollars? Why so much?"

"The judge is charging him with two counts of gun possession."

"But the guns are his legal guns; that does not make sense. Why can't you just release him?" "Well," the officer said, "because we cannot authenticate his second weapon."

"Well, then all you have to do is give him a ticket and if he does not appear in court, issue a warrant for his arrest." I went on to explain, "My son has never been arrested; he has no criminal record whatsoever."

The officer did not want to hear that.

"Okay," I said, "so the bail is hundred thousand dollars?"

"Yes," was his reply. I mentioned to my neighbor that would be ten thousand dollars, the officer overheard me and interrupted and said that this has to be paid in cash. I raised my voice.

"Cash? You want me to give you one hundred thousand dollars in cash? I don't have that kind of money."

"Well, you can go to a bail's bondsman, here is a name for you, he is not too far away."

As we were talking, I saw my son with two white police officers, his hands were in cuffs. I yelled "Where are you taking my son?"

The officer said, "Calm down, they are only taking him to be fingerprinted."

He told me if I did not bail him out by 11:30 PM he would be taken to the County. My heart sank. I did not want my son going to the County, especially in Elizabeth, NJ. Their jail had just had a serious incident with gangs from Mexico and I heard so many complaints about the Elizabeth jails. Union County is very racist. I was raised in Elizabeth, NJ. I did not realize the jails were so horrible. I did not want my son there. Also working in the prison system, I knew you could go into jail without a charge and come out with one because there are so many illegal things going on in jail. I overheard the officer calling the bails bondsman telling him you will probably have someone call you tonight. I did not know where I would get the money. I called a bondsman I knew, I told him what was going on. He said he needed ten thousand dollars. I asked him if he would take a credit card and he said no. I finally called the bondsman the police recommended. We went to Vauxhall, and met with the bondsman. Since the bail was one hundred thousand dollars, I put my house up as collateral. I paid ten thousand dollars, plus eight hundred and fifty dollars in processing fee. My house was valued at two hundred and fifty thousand dollars. I did not think about how I would pay the money back; I just wanted my son home. As I indicated earlier, my son had never been in trouble except for school fights, etc. He graduated from high school and wanted to be a correction officer. He wanted to be a police officer. He was twenty-five years old at the time. He was never a part of a gang. He is not a follower. He was gainfully employed, and I knew for a fact the guns the police confiscated were legal because I signed for him to get them, I knew he was innocent. I spent over twenty thousand dollars not knowing how I was going to get that money back. I wouldn't have put my only asset—my house—as collateral if believed my son was guilty. The thought of my son being locked up sickened me. My oldest son was already in jail, and having both my sons in jail, mentally, I could not take that pressure. It's better having him home fighting rather than have him inside the jail because I would worry about his safety. I did not want my son to come home an angry young man. I did the right thing, I said I am bringing my son home. Before my son was released, all kinds of things were going through my mind. I said to my neighbor I couldn't imagine what he was thinking about bringing his guns out like that. Then my neighbor said, "Let's hope the bullets are not hollow."

"What do you mean by that?" I said.

He said hollow bullets are worse than regular bullets and he could do more time because hollow bullets were designed as "killer cop" bullets.

"What! he would not be that stupid."

"Yeah, well it is good if you are getting him out because you may not be able to get him out if the bullets are hollow."

It was a dark night, but it got darker at that point. There is no way he would buy those kinds of bullets. I just shook my head, and said "lord, lord, lord." This was my first experience with a bail bondsman. The bondsman made a call to his assistant and within fifteen minutes, this guy came in the office with his machine. He told me the papers they would need to release my son. Once all documents were secured and the payment was made, my son would be released. We drove back to the police station, gave the documents to the lieutenant, and shortly thereafter, my son was released. We gave each other a big hug, a real big hug. He said "Thank you mommy, but you did not have to spend your money mommy" he just shook his head, "I know you don't have that kind of money. I'm going to pay you back."

I said, "I love you."

"I love you too mommy."

He thanked our neighbor for bringing me to the police station because my son knew I would not have found the place with my nerves being like they were—I would have gotten in an accident. My neighbor dropped us off at Kintock to pick up my car. My son and I got into the car and drove home. While we were driving, we talked about getting an attorney. He said he knew an attorney and would speak to them. Our neighbor who took me to pick up my son also referred me to his attorney. I was exhausted. I asked my son what happened. He told me the police pulled him over because his taillight was broken. When they pulled him over, they asked for his license, registration. Then they asked him to get out the car. He asked them why they were asking him to get out since he given them the documents. "Just get out," the police officer said. He complied with them. They began searching the car (which was illegal), and during the search they found the gun in his glove compartment. The police went crazy and told him to fall to the ground. As I was listening to my son tell his story, I was thinking about when he was growing up, I would tell him how to behave if he was ever stopped by the police. What to do, what to say. We are still telling our sons how to act if stopped by the police in 2019. I remember I heard Min. Farrakhan say one time how important it is for you to know what to do and how to act when the police pull you over. I was thinking to myself, *thank you father, my drilling that in him paid off.*

Then I asked where in Union was, he? He said it was a predominantly black area of Union and of course there were drugs in the area. But he was there meeting up with his friends. That's why they searched his car, he said, they thought he was a drug dealer because he fit the profile. Young black male with locks, riding in a car with smoked windows. He said, "Mommy they had no right searching my car. Then they searched my trunk and found my shotgun."

He said they thought that the guns were illegal until he showed them the permit to carry. "Yeah" I said, "and that probably made them mad, because they just assumed, the guns were illegal as most are with young black men in drug-infested areas."

Then he said they searched his car for drugs and didn't find any.

"Which probably made the police angrier," I said. "They probably said shit, this is a mistake there is no way this black man has a licensed gun and no drugs."

They locked him up just because. I asked if there were any black cops. He said no, they were all white. "Yeah," I said, "and I bet they were calling you nigga; nigga because they could not believe they arrested a smart young black man."

He laughed and said, "Yeah, you probably right." He started laughing.

I said, "What's so funny?" He said he was in the cell with drug dealers they looked at him and asked what he was in for, he told them, and they said, "Oh, they'll release you tonight, you don't have anything to worry about. Then when they found out what the police was charging him with, they said, if they did that to you, we're done. Cause it's obvious, you don't belong here. They started laughing he said, "I laughed too mommy."

"Well tomorrow we got to start looking for an attorney," I told him. We drove into the driveway, got in the house by 2 a.m. I took a quick shower, thanked God, and went to bed. I will deal with it later today I said to myself. I called my neighbor to thank him again for helping me. He said, "No problem, that's what friends are for." Me and my son got up the next day to pick his car up from the police pound in Kenilworth, NJ. We were just praying they did not destroy his car in any way. It cost me three hundred dollars to get his car out.

"Damn, more money. The system sure does make money off us," I said to my son. After I paid for his car, we went to pick it up. Thank God, they did not do anything to it. Then I was on my way to work. I was tired, but I am telling you, I was relieved too. It just felt good, I was a lot poorer, but I had my son. I was about to experience something, that would be a rude awakening for me. The next day my son found an attorney. He called to tell me about them. We met at their office about 4 p.m. in downtown Newark, NJ. The attorneys were white in their thirties and forties. They had a nice office on the ninth floor. We discussed the case. They said to me that they knew T had never been in jail, he's a high school graduate, from a nice home, and had a supportive mother; they said this case would be a piece of cake. As a matter of fact, I remember, they said, T is their first client they had who had never been in jail, had no record, he was perfect, and he should get off with no problem. I felt good hearing that. But I said, well suppose it does not happen like that. Then they said, they could get the mayor involved. My son and I looked at each other. "What mayor?" we said at the same time. "Cory Booker," she said excitingly.

T quickly said, "Why would you do that? You just said that I was the perfect candidate to be exonerated."

"Just in case," they said. I interjected and said "Listen, I am not impressed with Cory Booker, I did not vote for him and I do not need you to speak to him, because I know him and all the council members. I have been the school board president for Newark Public Schools. However, this is not a political arrest. Meaning, my son was not arrested for protesting some political policy, he was arrested because he was profiled for being black while driving in a drug-infested neighborhood. Now that could be political, but we are not going that route. If you are as good attorneys as you claim you are, you should not have no problem getting my son's case dismissed because that is what I want, and once his case was dismissed, I wanted to sue Union County."

They said we could do that, but we must first file a claim against Union County Police by going to Internal Affairs, requesting an investigation. T went to Internal Affairs about a week later. When he went there, I was nervous, because I just had this feeling, they would arrest him again. I did not feel comfortable until I saw my son again. Working with brothers and sisters who committed crimes, counseling them, developing a work-and-release plan and at the same time, trying to keep my son out of jail, keeping a clean record for him were one of the hardest things I ever had to do. I just did not know it was going to get harder in the days ahead. Well, we got a call from his attorney saying his arraignment was on Thursday, July 10, at the Union County Court House in Elizabeth. That Wednesday, I let my supervisor know I would be late the next day and if I did not come in, I would let her know because I had something personal to take care of. This was my first experience with this, and even though I had been working with ex-offenders, I did not know what to expect. I drove my car to work while my son followed. I parked my car at work, then I got into his car. We drove to the Elizabeth Court House. We parked his car, walked to the courthouse, waited outside for a while, and then they opened the doors for us to come in. We went through the metal detector and upstairs to the courtroom. We met his attorney; she told us we did not have to appear in court and that she could have pled not guilty on his behalf since she was representing him. I said nope, we are going to experience this from the beginning to the end. I wanted to experience this and wanted to know what was going on. They finally called my son's name. There were about twenty-five other people in the court including some inmates who were in custody they were standing behind the windows with the Union County Sheriffs. My son and his attorney appeared in front of the judge.

"How do you plead?" she asked.

"Not guilty," was my son's attorney's response.

"Mr. Bey," the judge said, "you do realize you are released on bail and if you do not appear in court your bail will be revoked, and a warrant will be issued for your arrest. Do you understand?" "Yes Honor," he said.

"You will appear in court on September 1st at 9 a.m."

It took less than five minutes.

"That's it?" I said to the attorney.

"That's it," she said.

"You know, you did not have to pay all that money and put your house up for your son. He could have stayed in the County because he has never been in trouble, and his bail would have been an easy thousand dollars or less."

"Yeah, you are probably right I said, but suppose he got into trouble while he was in jail, he could have gotten a new charge, right?"

She agreed. You see, I was not taking that chance with my son's life. After the arraignment, our attorney told us we had to go to the basement for processing. We got to the basement; it was crowded with so many people. We found the spot and were told T had to see a secretary to fill out the paperwork. We went to the secretary's office. She asked for T's driver's license. He asked why she needed it, her response was "We have to create a file on you, we will need to take your fingerprints and mug shot," I said, "WHAT?! He has not been found guilty."

"Yes, you are right Ms. Bey, but he was arrested, and he has a pending case, this is our procedure."

I saw my son's face just drop. He said "Man, now this will be on my record." The secretary said only until the case is complete and hopefully the charges dismissed. You will get a call from your attorney letting you know your next court appearance. I said "Son, it is going to be alright as long as we have each other." He just shook his head. I wanted to cry. We walked out of the courthouse not saying a word. It was a clear day, but I could not tell because tears were streaming down my face and looking at my son just made it worse. His face was tight and drawn he was just shaking his head. We walked to the parking lot to pick up his car. He drove me back to work. There was silence in the car, he looked distraught. I was devastated. I looked at him and told him everything was going to be alright again. I did not like this. The only focus I had now was getting my son free. Parents who have gone through this know what I am talking of. My goal was to support him and let him know I loved him. I went back to work. I walked into my office and prayed. I said, "God only you can get us through this. Please Father be with my son, keep him strong, and Father, we cannot do it without you, Amen." My nerves were getting shocked, I did not know how much of this I could take. It seems like when it rains it pours. Now I was having a "pity party." You know how we do. I started thinking about the good paying job I lost two years ago, working on a job paying half of what I made, bills have not changed (you know how it goes), and now this. I closed my blinds because I did not want the residents to see me crying. They would have gotten concerned and worried. I got through the day and went home and just fell in my bed. My son came upstairs later to see how I was doing. He said, I am going to pay you back. "I know," I said.

But he said, "Mommy I told you not to bail me out, I could have stayed in the county, and it would have been cheaper, I know you don't have money."

I said "Listen, I love you, I am glad I was able to get you out of jail. God gave us this house for a reason, he knew this would happen one day. I am in more debt, but you are home, and trust me, if you were guilty, where would your butt be sitting right now?"

He said, "In jail."

"That's right. But I know you are innocent and am so thankful to God that I could bring you home. You see, getting you out was for my own peace of mind. I would have been working and worrying about you. So, I did it for me as much as I did it for you."

He smiled and said, "I love you."

"Me too," I said. We hugged. He went back downstairs. I got out of my bed and went to the bathroom to take a quick, hot shower—it was so soothing. I really needed that. I put on my PJ's, jumped in my bed, and went to sleep in less than fifteen minutes. The next day I went to work and, of course, my son was on my mind. He went to work. He had been working as a security guard. He wanted to be a police officer and work in law enforcement, which is why he was so adamant about not having a record. I was happy to be working with brothers and sisters behind the walls, they helped me to get through my ordeal. They did not know my frustration or what I was going through with my son. I went to work as if everything was fine; when I came home, I broke down, I would not let my son see me—I knew it would hurt him. We tried to be as normal as possible and went about our daily routine. Finally, we received a call from our attorney informing us my son was to be in court August 3rd, appearing in front of Judge Triasi. I called my girlfriend Donna P. that evening and she said a prayer for us. She told me to say the Lord's Prayer when

I walked into the courtroom. We got up early. Even though Elizabeth, NJ, is not far from Newark, we did not want to take a chance on being late. We drove through Weequahic Park which took us to Elizabeth. There was not too much traffic. As I got closer to the courthouse, I remember what my girlfriend said to do. As we entered the courthouse, I silently chanted The Lord's Prayer. We were in court before 9 a.m. At 9:10, they called my son.

"Mr. Bey here, Your Honor," was his response. Just being inside that court made me sick but I had to be with my son. He was not going through this nightmare by himself. His lawyer came in a few minutes after my son's name was called. He had a female and male attorney. Today, it was the male attorney. He asked us to come outside so we could confer on things. I did not think we had to discuss anything because he was pleading not guilty. We went out to the hallway. The attorney explained this should be simple.

"Oh good," I said. We went back in the courtroom. I sat down in the front and observed all the County Sheriffs in the courtroom—they were there to keep the people in order. Always dress professional in situations like this—people treat you respectfully. For those of you who have been in court, you know they call those who have an attorney first. They called my son; he and his attorney went before the judge.

"How do you plead?" asked the judge.

"Not guilty," Your Honor. The judge was silent, he was looking at my son's paperwork, and then he looked up and said, "If you do not plead guilty, the next time you come before me, I will give you five extra years for each gun."

"What?" I stood up in the courtroom.

My son and his attorney looked at me.

I said, "Your Honor, you don't understand; those are his legal guns, they are not illegal guns, they are his guns."

There were County Sheriffs in the courtroom, but they did not say anything to me; they did not ask me to sit down or anything like that. The judge looked at my son and his attorney and said, "Who is that?"

My son said, "That's my mother."

"I repeat, if you do not plead guilty, I will add an additional five years for each gun. What are you going do?" the judge asked.

My son, his attorney, and I simultaneously said, "Not guilty."

"Okay," the judge said, "see you next month."

We walked out the courtroom, stunned. I could not believe what I had heard. I asked the attorney if the judge was drunk.

"I thought you said it's going to be easy."

"No," he said, "if you noticed Ms. Bey everyone who appeared before the judge took a plea—that's what they were hoping we would do. Before we take a plea, we will take it to trial he said. Don't worry T, it's going to be alright, you are going to be alright. Ms. Bey, it's is going to be alright. These judges try to scare you into taking pleas and if you notice, all those people had records, T did not. He had legal guns and he should not plead guilty for carrying his guns."

"You're right," I said. Well, that day I was just too through with that judge, so much so I did not return to work. Instead, I went home and wrote a letter to the Attorney General on that judge. I got a response from the Attorney General, saying that we would have to let it work itself out in our court system. This is the letter:

September 12, 2007
Anne Milgram,
Attorney General
Trenton, New Jersey

Dear Ms. Milgram:

By now I am certain you have heard of the Jena Six case in Jena Louisiana. I have had this letter on my computer since August 4, 2007. I am the mother of Mr. Bey who is a 25-year-old young black man that was arrested Saturday, June 23, 2007. I have hesitated to write this letter because my son has private attorneys representing him. However, after seeing you on the Record and Learning of the Jena Case, I felt compelled to write you because my son's freedom is at stake. On Saturday, June 23, 2007, my son was arrested by the Union Township Police. Upon my arrival to the police department, I was informed my son had been arrested for carrying his licensed firearms. I informed the policeman that I was aware my son had firearms and that he had purchased them legally. That evening, I had to secure my property in order for my son to be released on a $100,000 bail for two counts of unlawful possession of firearms that he owned. My son was obviously upset with the arrest. I told him that once he appears before the judge, the case should be dismissed. Considering he had all his documents to support ownership. I felt it would be a fair decision. How wrong was I. On Thursday, August 2, 2007, my son appeared before Judge John Triarsi. Though my son provided proof that he legally purchased the guns, Judge Triarsi threatened my son that if he did not plead guilty to the unlawful possession of firearms and accept probation, at the next hearing the years of incarceration would increase to 3 to 5 per gun. I could not believe this judge. I yelled out in the courtroom to the judge that those guns were his and purchased legally. Ms. Milgram, my son and I understand the concern of illegal guns, the need to have tighter gun control, and that illegal guns are destroying many of our neighborhoods. My son acted responsibly. He purchased his guns legally. Ms.

Milgram, my son has never been in jail. He had no criminal record, but thanks to the Union Township Police Department and Judge Triarsi, he has an arrest record. I cannot believe that Judge Triarsi overlooked the fact that my son owned his guns and that he (Triarsi) wants my son to go to jail. Had this been a white 25-year-old man, this case would have been dismissed possibly with a fine. For my son to be arrested and jailed is absolutely ridiculous. I have taught my son to respect the law. I have successfully raised him to stay away from drug dealers and gang members so that he would not go to jail. I did not raise him to be criminalized by this criminal justice system. I taught him how to act if the police approached him, and to know his rights. He is a law-abiding citizen. He has worked in law enforcement; his dream job is to become an armed guard. A dream that may be deferred if Judge Triarsi has anything to say about it. On August 2nd, the men and women who appeared before this Judge Triarsi had records or extensive records of some kind. My son was the only defendant who had no record. Where is the justice? What is wrong with this judge? Bottom line, Ms. Milgram, my son was racially profiled by Union Township Police and Judge Triarsi. I am requesting an investigation by your office of Judge Triarsi and the Union Township Police Department. You see, Ms. Milgram, the Township of Union and Judge Triarsi is my JENA SIX. As his mother, I view this behavior by the Union Township Police Department and particularly Judge Triarsi as the CRIMINALIZATION OF BLACK MEN. I am sure that once this case is exposed, you will no doubt have more complaints regarding the criminalization of our good children by this system. Finally, this arrest appears on record checks when my son applies for employment. Why? I look forward to hearing from you. Thank you for taking the time to read this letter.

Sincerely,
Maryam Bey, Mother

Cc: Governor Jon Corzine, Senator Frank Lautenberg,
US Senate Congressman Donald Payne, Senator Ronald Rice

I received a call from Senator Ronald Rice; he wanted to know what he could do. I had worked as a coordinator on Senator Rice's campaign, plus my son worked with him as well. We have known Senator Rice for years, so we got a supportive call from him. Governor Corzine sent a letter via his assistant, and there was no response from Congressman Donald Payne. Bottom line, nothing was done—or so I thought. Our next court appearance was in front of another judge. We did not appear before that crazy judge's court again. Thank God. For one year, we went back and forth to court. We did not miss one court date. My son would say "Mommy, you do not have to come to court all the time." "Oh yes, I do." I would tell him. You see, I wanted to be there for him, and I wanted them to see that he has family support. That makes a difference, it does. When the court representatives see that you are not by yourself, they know there will be some fight back, so yes it makes a difference. Going back and forth with so many crazy episodes of nonsense, we never thought about pleading. It was so astonishing to me how the courts, who are predominately white, were criminalizing our Black and Hispanic children. It was equally shocking and amazing that for one year, whenever my son would appear before a judge, he was the only defendant who did not have a record, the only one who had never been in jail, the only defendant who was not addicted to drugs or alcohol, and the only defendant who had not robbed or stolen from anyone. Yet, the courts wanted to criminalize my son. That infuriated me, and I was so tired. But I made it to every court hearing. I remember one day, my son received a call from his attorney, which I did not know. Thank God he told me. He said "Mommy, my attorney called and said I did not have to come to court today."

I asked him, "Why did the secretary call to let you know not to be in court today?" He said he did not know.

"We are going to court," I said. "**<u>The judge does not want</u>** to see your attorney, he wants to see you and if you are not in that court room, you will be in contempt and I will lose my house, let's go."

We got to the court at about 9:15, they had not called anyone yet. At about 10, they began calling names, they called my son. I looked at him. Now if you were not supposed to be here, why did the clerk call your name? If you were not here, a warrant would have been issued for your arrest. He just shook his head. To make matters worse, his attorney was late. As a matter of fact, his attorneys began making it a habit of being late. We stayed in the court all morning. The judge wondered where our attorney was. My son said he had no idea. The judge asked his clerk to get our attorney on the phone. The clerk got her and asked why she was not there. She responded saying she was under the impression it was rescheduled.

"Who told you that?" the judge asked. He gave us another court date and he left the courtroom upset with the attorney. Before we left, I asked the prosecutor what would have happened if my son had not appeared. Though the clerk told us what would happen, I wanted my son to hear it from the prosecutor. The prosecutor responded by saying, "A warrant would have been issued for your son's arrest and your home would have been seized." My son and I just looked at each other and shook our heads, because we knew that almost happened. Some of you may be asking the question at this time, "What does my son's arrest have to do with "broken spirit"? This chapter is important, as my son could have become a "broken spirit"; for a while he was because of his current circumstances. We all are at some point in our lives discouraged. The reality was were it not for the fact that he had a supportive parent, who happened to have some knowledge of the system, who also happened to own property that was used as collateral to bail him out of jail, and who had access to resources and friends, the outcome would have been different. The unfortunate thing I learned is that most average people do not know or have resources available to them and most people do not know that information empowers them. So, at that moment, my son was becoming a **broken spirit**. He however had friends and family who believed in his innocence, this worked in his favor. Another reason why this chapter is important is that we must prevent the criminal justice system from criminalizing our children and turning them into "broken spirits." This ordeal took us to several visits with his attorneys regarding numerous issues. I sat in those courtrooms and witnessed the attempted criminalization of my son, and I did not like it. I was thankful I knew something about the law, and I was so thankful for my house. I was proud of how my son was handling this situation because it could have "turned for the worse". My son came to me one morning and said, "Mommy, if it were not for you, I would not have made it this far, thank you." I said, "You are welcome, and I am happy I was in a position to help, and even though financially it's hurting me, your freedom is more important to me." Again, he said he would pay me back and I just smiled. To all the parents out there, we know when our children say they will pay us back, in more cases than none, we will not get that money back. I just smiled again, because my son was home with me. This was my first experience with the court system with my youngest son who was innocent. My oldest son served time in prison. I was never involved in his cases because the criminal lifestyle was something he chosen. So, this experience was new to me. Though I worked with inmates as an Employment Counselor, Case Manager, and Consultant. I had never experienced the court system as a mother trying to save her son. A situation that should have been a low court charge, which is a municipal charge, escalated into a high court, grand jury charge. For sure, as I mentioned earlier, if my son had been a young white man, this would have never happened. That is a fact. We still live in a country that profiles our young black men and views them as criminals. We went through this tribulation one year. It was the worst year of my life. The constant reminder that my son could have been convicted for carrying his legal guns was outrageous. We were sent from high court to municipal court, then back to high court. We sat in those courtrooms from 9 a. m. to 4 p.m. sometimes twice a month. Maybe it was due to our attorney not showing up or the judge having to alter his calendar. Maybe they were hoping we would not show up—I am sure the thought was there. Had we not shown up, my son would have gone to jail and I would have lost my home. Though he was innocent of one charge, he becomes guilty of another, contempt of court, you know not showing up. The criminal justice system is out to get our children. It is about the money. This experience scared me. When my son is not home and the phone would ring, I get nervous. Though this was 13 years ago. Anyway, one of most troublesome incidents related to his case was when my son was applying for employment, the arrest record was highlighted, meaning he could not be considered for the position of law enforcement until his case was dismissed. As a matter of fact, his case had to be dismissed since he was planning to work in law enforcement. So, for one year, the only money coming in our home was my income and that hurt us. All bills were paid by my income and rental income, which meant many bills did not get paid. I just put it in God's hands because I was doing all I could do. Eventually, my son became depressed because of what he was experiencing. He came to me several times when we were going through this and said, "Mommy I could not make this without you, thank you." You know," he said, "I now understand why people take pleas." I said "Yeah, but we are not taking a plea. This is going to be dismissed; we just have got to stay strong and keep the faith." He told me he saw his former supervisor who heard what happened to him. He told my son that it is not what you go through, but how you come out of it or end up. Will you be better for the experience, will you learn from it, or will you be broken? (I remember saying something like that to J in the previous chapter). That's important. My son said he thought about me when his former supervisor made the statement. Working with inmates during this challenge in my life helped me get through it. It helped me help them. This experience with my son was a blessing to other inmates because I learned so much about the system. This experience allowed me to tell inmates to not take pleas if they are innocent. However, that statement would lead to a discussion about support. Such as family and finances. Many inmates did not have parents or family members who came to court, nor did they have finances or resources. We discussed other types of support they could get. It also gave me the opportunity to lecture on what their responsibilities were, and the reality was they would be home had they not committed crimes for whatever the reasons—most agreed. However, I would remind them that the reality is, this is a racist society that has two laws—one for whites and one for blacks and Latinos—and for sure if you do not have money, the system is slow in responding. I expressed to the inmates during my lectures that when you go through any life-challenging adversities and you grow through them, you are learning from that experience; if you are successful in the experience, you become a testimony for someone else. I believed that one day

I was going to tell this story to someone because someone else will go through what my son and I went through. It was important my son win his case. You know it was revealing how this system beats you down to get you to plead your case. I remember the prosecutor would come to my son on a regular basis and ask him if he wanted to plead to a lesser crime and take PTI (pre-trial intervention). We said no and I asked what was PTI. I did not know at the time, but it's when you plead guilty to a lesser charge, you receive probation for one year, (in my son's case), and if you do not get arrested within that period of time, your charge is expunged (removed). I mentioned to the prosecutor, if my son does that, he is admitting he's guilty when he's not. PTI is good for first-time offenders who are guilty, but I did not want PTI for my son he was innocent. The prosecutor came to us each time we appeared in court with that option and each time we said no. My son's attorney also suggested he should consider PTI. This is my son's attorney who originally implied T was their model client. There are some attorneys who does work with courts to criminalize our children though they are being paid by the client. As matter of fact, one of my son's attorneys admitted they had to do PTI at one time in their life, my son replied, "Yeah, that's because you were guilty, I am not guilty." Going back and forth to court was an eye-opener. In court one day, I mentioned to the attorney "Is it necessary for me to contact Rev. Al Sharpton?" They said, "Oh no, that is not necessary, we can defend your son." I said, "Well, this is really taking long." I did contact Rev. Sharpton, but it was a waste. I did not let the attorneys know that I contacted Rev. Sharpton's office because they really looked concerned that he might get involved. However, I did not believe he would because it seems Rev. Sharpton's organization only respond to cases that are high profile. That's in the news. I believed if my son had been shot or killed, Rev. Sharpton or his office would have responded. However, this was not a sensational case—no cameras, no demonstrations, just a young black man who had never been in trouble and his mother only trying to prevent her son from becoming another victim of the system, another "broken spirit." I informed his attorney that I would get character letters on my son's behalf and that might help. I reached out to people who knew my son, who watched him grow up, who knew me when I was pregnant with him. I did not ask strangers. I was shocked by one sister's response. She asked me what were his charges? I let her know, it was a gun charge and that the guns were his legally and that he had a permit to carry. I assured her that if he was not guilty, I would never ask her to write a letter. I had known this sister for more than thirty years. There was silence on the other end. She said she would get back to me, she had to speak to her daughter. Well, she did get back to me, but the response was no, her daughter felt she should not get involved. I said thank you. Now mind you, this sister asked me and members in the community to write letters for brothers in prison who we did not know and sign petitions for her friends who were coming home from prison. The fact that she knew them was enough for us to write a support letter. However, she refused to write a letter for a young man she personally knew all his life and had never experienced the prison system. That was shocking to me. He was arrested for carrying his two legal guns. Maybe she felt he was guilty and just did not want to say that to me. So, the excuse was, her daughter felt she should not get involved. I said thank you, and kept it moving. Because we know there will be some who wouldn't be supportive when something like this happens. So, there is no reason to get mad. It shows you who will support you in times of trouble and who will not. We were fortunate that I have been a community activist all my life, a PTA President, a school board member, a school board president, worked for the city of Newark, chaired, and developed numerous conferences, and was affiliated with many organizations, so I knew a lot of people, but I did not want a hundred letters, I only wanted those who knew my son intimately. Strategically, I thought that would be the best way to handle this situation. When people write letters about you and they know you, it makes a difference. I asked his coach, two of his teachers, and two Newark council members. All of them responded with a resounding yes and asked what I wanted them to do. I asked them to write a letter to the judge and how they knew my son. When the letters were given to the attorneys, they were impressed, when the letters were read by the judge and prosecutor, they were equally impressed. I think after reading the five letters, they realized they were dealing with a young man who had a lot going for him. He was not the typical young man and woman that usually appeared in their court. He was twenty-five years old, a high school graduate, employed, no children, and no drug or criminal history. I Included three of the five letters at the end of this chapter. I tell this story to inmates during my lectures. There are some inmates who are innocent, and they need to hear that they should not take a plea unless they are guilty. Some would say, "Well, Ms. Bey, I just want to get home to my family, that's why I pled guilty." "Yeah," would be my reply, "and now you have a felony." They would just shake their head and say, "You're right, Ms. Bey."

Two things happened after the character letters were given to the judge and prosecutor. We were asked one more time if we wanted PTI, and of course I said no to the prosecutor. The second thing happened was in December 2007; a prosecutor read my son's case and went to the judge and stated to the judge that this was a young man who had a bright future ahead of him, and he wanted to join law enforcement. The prosecutor continued by saying that he did not want to destroy this young's man life. They wanted to work something out. The judge asked us to return to court in January 2008. We returned in January and went back and forth. We had to go back in February, in March, in April, and finally in May 2008, the case was dismissed. I gave a sigh of relief, hugged my son, and made a few phone calls. I then went home, cried a little bit, prayed a little bit, and just thanked God for helping us through this one. There was a minor setback for about a week. When I looked at the dismissal, the judge had not signed it, and therefore, the case was not really dismissed. I immediately called the attorney, he said not to worry, the judge would sign it next week. I worried.

"Suppose the judge dies?" I said.

"Calm down, Ms. Bey, we can fix this," the attorney stated.

The next week the papers were signed by the judge. And the following week after getting the papers from the bail's bondmen, I took the papers to the Essex County Registrar in Newark, NJ, my home was returned to me, and my son returned to work. Below are three of the five Character letters written for my son.

MILDRED C. CRUMP
PRESIDENT · MUNICIPAL COUNCIL
NEWARK, NEW JERSEY 07102

CITY HALL ROOM 304
920 BROAD STREET
NEWARK, NEW JERSEY 07102
(973) 733-8043

November 19, 2007

Re: Tiharka Bey

To Whom It May Concern:

I am pleased to write this letter of character reference for the above- noted individual. I have known him since the approximate age of 12 years. Even then, he demonstrated those characteristics and behaviors of one who was destined to lead a life of service to his community. He and his mother traveled with me to various community meetings and events. He was always interested and listened attentively to the concerns expressed.

I have had the pleasure of watching him grow and develop into a young man of purpose and promise. The promise is what I saw in him as a young man. The purpose is the manner in which he now conducts himself. He is not idle in word or deed. He has proven to be the outstanding young man I always believed him to be. He is an asset to his family and community. His capacity has yet to be fully comprehended. I expect even greater things from him. I am proud to count him a member of my extended family.

If you have any further questions, please feel free to contact me.

Yours truly,

Mildred C. Crump

Mildred C. Crump
President,
Newark Municipal Council

RONALD C. RICE
COUNCIL MEMBER - WEST WARD
NEWARK, NEW JERSEY 07102

CITY HALL ROOM 304
920 BROAD STREET
NEWARK, NEW JERSEY 0710
(973) 733-6427

October 25, 2007

To Whom It May Concern:

I am writing this correspondence as a personal testament to the character and integrity of Mr. Taharqa Bey. I have personally known Taharqa since he was a child and have watched him overcome great odds to become a young man that is not only committed to making a difference in his community of birth, but in also pursuing a career in law enforcement to serve the community as his chosen vocation.

Taharqa has never been arrested, indicted, convicted, or even suspected of committing any type of criminal acts in his past and I am completely perplexed, based on what I know of this case, over this current situation for which he is being persecuted.

I am aware that your court receives countless letters of reference supporting many that come before you. Indeed, I have written a few for others myself. Unlike those previous testaments, I am writing this one on behalf of Taharqa based on personal observation, interaction, and working with him to be a part of the law enforcement community in the city of Newark as he represents our best and brightest stars.

It is my deepest hope that this letter will be taken in the context of how it has been composed: as a serious attempt to positively persuade your court to remedy these charges in a manner that will allow the continued ascendancy of a young man that strives to be great and to be a giver, not a taker, in the neighborhood of his birth and maturation.

Please feel free to contact my office with any questions and/or concerns you may have regarding this correspondence.

Thanking you for your anticipated careful consideration and attention, I remain,

Sincerely,

Ronald C. Rice

Ronald C. Rice
West Ward Councilman
City of Newark, New Jersey

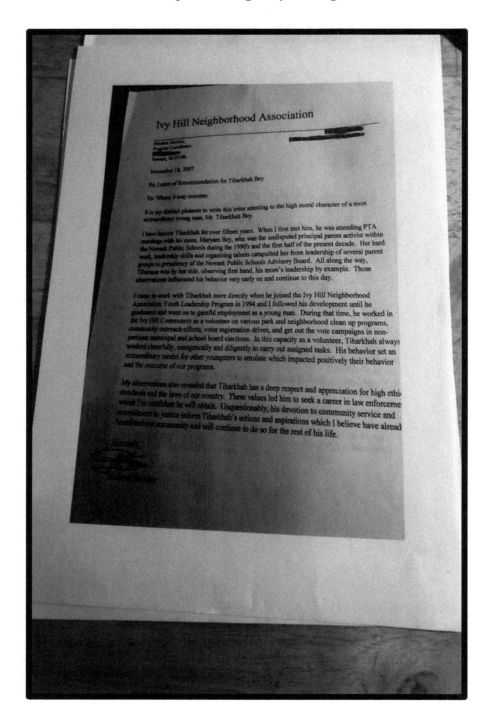

T and me

<u>IF EYES COULD KILL</u>

This incident was such a revelation to me concerning an individual's interpretation of how he believed I observed him or what I thought of him. This was a young man who became infuriated when I informed the group that I would critique the written assignment given to them for discussion. At the time, I didn't realize how potentially dangerous this situation could have been if I hadn't handled it from a nonjudgmental and lack-of-fear position. This was a group discussion on how to handle conflict. A scenario was given to the group, after which they were asked to write their interpretation of the situation. Once their papers were given to me, I read the papers, made my corrections or suggestions on their paper, and at the next group I returned their assignments to them and asked them to redo their paper with my changes.

Honestly, I was not prepared for this resident's reaction. He came to my office with his paper and said to me he did not like how I marked up his paper. I answered with, "It's not marking, it's corrections or suggestions." He felt I was "dissing" him (disrespecting). I asked him to have a seat. I explained to him it was not my intention to disrespect him but to improve the quality of his writing assignment. He wasn't buying it. He felt I was humiliating him. WOW, I said to myself. I have to handle this with thoughtful sensitivity. I had to make sure I did not give him the impression I thought he was stupid because it could have gotten ugly. I saw the anger in his eyes and observed his body language. I got the feeling this had happened before, and it didn't turn out in his best interest. I looked in his eyes and reassured him very bluntly that I was not dissing him. I said to him I would not want anyone to do that to me. I asked him to follow my instructions on the paper as I suggested. I gave him more writing papers, which he took; however, I could see he was still offended. If eyes could kill or if he had a gun at that moment, I would have been dead. I showed no fear and was very firm in my expectations of what I was requesting him to turn in. I asked him again, if he would please do that for me and he will understand my point. I reminded him we would discuss this in the group. Finally, I said to him I was not trying to hurt him and that I only wanted the best for him. He left my office. When he left, I thought about what just happened. I shook my head, breathed a sigh of relief, and thanked God for his protection. My mind flashed to a scene in *Training Day* with Denzel Washington when he says "You wanna go to jail or you wanna go home?"

"I wanna go home," I said to myself. Whenever conflicting issues happen to me at work and I do not have the answers, I bring them home with me, as many caring and concerned counselors and teachers do. I thought about this inmate's response to the assignment. I processed the entire incident and came up with this: this had to have happened to him in the past with someone he trusted. Then it hit me. "Tomorrow when I get to my office, I would look at his education history." The next morning, I got to my office and went to the file cabinet. I took out his file and read his educational history. He was a Newark resident who dropped out of school in the tenth grade. He was twenty-five years old. It was all making sense to me now. I looked at the clock; I had fifteen minutes before the group started. I gathered my thoughts and decided I would change the format and rather than asking them to turn in their papers we would have a discussion on "critiquing." Before I began the group, I asked them how many of them had completed the assignment. There were thirty-five inmates in the group. Majority raised their hands. The rest had not completed the assignment. I began the group. I asked those who completed the assignment to hold their papers and those who did not complete the assignment to listen carefully. I asked them if they knew what the root word of "critique" was.

One brother raised his hand and said "critical," and another brother asked, "What is a root word?" I said to the brother who answered my question that he was half-right and smiled. To the other brother, I said "Good question." I looked at the brother who was angry with me yesterday—he didn't look that angry. I gave them the definition of a root word. Then we had our discussion on critique and its root word. Simply put, I informed them, critiquing in one example is a form of criticizing, judging, making a person feel bad or embarrassed, depending on the situation.

"Like in the streets or in school, if a friend says something about you and you believe they are disrespecting you or finding fault in you, the outcome could be an argument, a fight, or something deadly if you do not discuss what the intentions were—you know an explanation, right?"

They agreed. However, I said to them, critiquing is also a form of improving the work you are doing. I gave them the example of going over things over and over again. "What does that do?" I asked them. Their response, "It makes you better." I asked them if they saw the scene in the *Temptation* movie, where the group had to perform in front of Motown's founder Barry Gordy. They all said yes.

"Okay," I said, "before they auditioned for him, they had to do what?"

"Practice," they responded.

"Right," I replied. "In practicing they were doing what?"

One brother said, "critiquing their moves and singing."

"Right," I said, "and in doing so it improved the quality of their performance so much that they were offered a contract with Motown."

This discussion gave me the opportunity to mention to them that when I critique their papers, I am improving the quality of their writing and what they are expressing in their written assignments.

"I am not disrespecting you or hurting you; I am helping you."

I reviewed the definitions of critique again: 1) critical, disrespectful, negative, fault finding and 2) improvement, quality, understanding. I said to them now that we got that out of the way, I want you to go over your papers, correct them, and return them to me. I also informed them that when I was in college, my English professor applied the same methods to his students resulting in us becoming better writers. Later, that afternoon, the young man whose looks could kill came to my office and apologized to me for misinterpreting my intentions. I thanked him and said to him, "I didn't take it personally," "I was concerned with your reaction and I am happy you finally understood my intentions were authentic.

"I was pursuing answers to your response. It could have turned out a different way, as it does in the streets most of the time, and all we can say is 'I'm sorry,' but then it's too late."

"You're right, Ms. Bey, I apologize again."

"No problem," I said. "Have a good day and get your assignment to me."

He smiled and walked out the door. What society does to our children is criminalized their behaviors rather than address negative behaviors. Their attitude leads to the incarcerating of our children.

EDUCATE, INVOKE, STIMULATE

When I was a counselor at Delaney Hall, I showed these documentaries to residents. I wanted residents to understand the trajectory of incarceration and why prisons were essential to the economy of America and why it was compulsory for White America to use African American slaves free labor to build America during slavery. I also wanted residents to understand that when slaves were "so called freed", all slaves had a trade. I showed Hidden Colors by Tariq Nasheed about the untold history of people of African and Aboriginal descent and Slavery by Another Name, author, Douglas A Blackmon. As an educator, I realize the importance of all people knowing their history. When I showed these documentaries to residents, Black, White, Hispanic, their response was, "wow, I didn't know". Or "I had to come to prison to learn my history". This gave me the opportunity to remind residents we all have a history, good or bad and no one is perfect. The discussions were passionate as well as soulful. They were free to express themselves if it were respectful. Most residents have not had a discussion on this level without some sort of negative confrontation or hostility. I would remind them we do not have to kill each other because we disagree. They would respond, "you right Ms. Bey". The reasons, I loved working at Delaney Hall, Kintock and Essex County Correctional Facility is they provided me the opening to use and maximize skills to empower residents thought practices invoking a consciousness of respect for themselves. I will always appreciate these institutions for that opportunity. As I mentioned in the original Broken Spirit Let It Go So You Can Grow, my goal was to illustrate to residents/inmates how they participated in their incarceration and that it was a set-up.

Finally, I know we have good cops, but they must come forward and stop the silence. When cops kill, they render children fatherless, and wives' widows. There is a consequence to silence.

"Our lives begin to end the day we become silent about things that matter." "In the end, we will remember not the words of our enemies, but the silence of our friends."

Dr. Martin Luther King, Jr.

Another quote by Dr. King "Injustice anywhere is a threat to justice everywhere." Dr. Martin Luther King, Jr.

BAD HAIR DAY (BUCKWHEAT)

As an Employment Counselor, my responsibilities were to obtain employment for inmates once they passed the employment test. Resumes were created for them, we conducted mock interviews, so residents would feel confident during their interview. Sometimes they would have their own clothes or sometimes we referred them to an agency that provided professional clothing. The program was called "Dress for Success"—the same agency I used for the fifty-year-old who had never worked. Many of these brothers and sisters had not worked for many years and several of them were nervous about the thought of sitting in front of an interviewer. We also went over the process of filling out job applications. I emphasized the importance of appropriate attire and arriving at least fifteen minutes prior to the interview. In this group was a twenty-three-year-old male resident who did not have a care in the world. He had an entitlement attitude. I confirmed an interview for him at Popeye's Restaurant in Hillside, NJ. Two days prior, I called him into my office to let him know his interview was at 9:00 a.m. I reminded him to be properly dressed. I left his pass at the front desk so he would not have any problems departing the facility. I just happened to come to work a few minutes earlier the next day and saw him walking out the door on his way to the interview. I was shocked. I asked him where was he going? He said to the interview. I said not looking like that. He asked what was wrong with it. I requested he come to my office. He reluctantly returned to the building; he was upset because he knew he would not be leaving the building this day. When he got to the office, I asked him why he was dressed like that.

"Like what?" he said.

"Like that."

"A sweat suit that is three times bigger than you and gold sneakers, really? This is not casual wear for an interview," I said. "And look at your hair."

"What's wrong with my hair?" he stated.

"You didn't look in the mirror?" I asked him.

"No, I didn't."

"Well, it tells," I said. "You are not going on an interview today."

Most of the brothers get seriously upset when they are not allowed to go out, and trust me, this brother was upset but he was not leaving the building today. I asked him to have a seat and explained to him why I could not allow him to walk out the door looking like that.

"You want to work?"

"Yes," he said.

"Well, the way you are dressed gives the impression you want to rob someone. Your sweat suit is three times bigger than you are and you are wearing sneakers. Let me ask you a question. Are you familiar with the character Buckwheat in the Little Rascals?"

He said "Yeah." I said, "Well, your hair looks like Buckwheat's." I told him he was not walking out there. "Looking like that you'll scare somebody." He left the office mad. In the next fifteen minutes, I received a call from the Director asking me if he could come to my office. I said sure. The Director came in my office and proceeded to tell me how upset the resident was that he would not go on the interview. I said, "He's right, he's not going."

"Well Ms. Bey, what can we do to get him out on that interview?" he asked me.

"Proper interview attire?" I responded. "He will not leave this building looking like Buckwheat." "Okay, Ms. Bey, I agree with you. Can we call him to your office?"

"Of course," I said. I paged him to my office. In about five minutes, there was a knock on my door—it was the resident in that same oversized gold sweat suit, with the Buckwheat hair. I just wanted to shake him, but all I could do was just stare at him. The director explained to him that we wanted him to go on his interview, since Ms. Bey is your Employment Counselor, she is not allowing you to leave the building looking like that.

"So, Ms. Bey will give you instructions on what she wants you do.

The resident responded, "Okay."

I asked him to go into his room to get a pair of pants that fit and a decent shirt.

"Would he then be okay to go on the interview?" the director asked.

"No, he has to fix his hair and take those sneakers off, once he does that, he can go on the interview. But he can't leave the building until I see him— it's just that simple."

The director asked the resident if he understood the instructions.

"Yes," was his response.

About a half an hour later, he returned to my office. He looked much better, except for his hair. I could not take it. I asked the resident's permission to fix his hair. Once I combed his hair, he was ready for the interview. I told him he looked handsome, and he smiled. The director was pleased as well. I mentioned to the resident that my decision was not changing even though he informed the Director, he was not leaving the building looking like one of the Little Rascals. I gave him permission to go on the interview. He responded with a "thank you." He returned to building that afternoon and stopped by the office to apologize for his behavior and stated he appreciated I cared enough to not allow him to leave looking the way he did and that when he changed, he did feel better about himself. "Good," I said, "plus I did not want you to scare the staff at Popeye's." He laughed. "I will see you later." He said, "Okay, Ms. Bey." He did not get the job, which he knew he would not, because he did not have the right attitude. I discussed attitude with him as I do with all my clients, because to me "attitude" is everything. You know, a positive attitude will get you in the door a negative attitude will throw you out. He could have gotten the job because this company hired our residents. However, in his case, as with a lot of residents who are released from prison, their attitude needs serious adjustment. **This is why addressing behavior is so important.**

ADMINISTRATION AND NEGATIVE EMPLOYEES
Tactics Used to Break Inmates' Spirits
Most inmates, when they arrive at a halfway house or therapeutic treatment center or any prison facility, are broken spirits. Many are angry and mad at the world and have been broken down by society. There are various reasons why they are in this situation. The first person they are introduced to in the system once they are assigned to a room is the counselor. Prior to seeing a counselor some inmates have been treated in a humiliating manner so the remedy in their mind is to take it out on counselors. Desperation and immediate gratification are what they know. Counselors or Case Managers must interview inmates, get personal information, and determine how long they will stay in the facility. Their responses determine which programs they will be placed in while at the halfway house. Some men can be quite intimidating because of their physique and they can be scary—especially to women counselors. However, that behavior does not work with me. My philosophy is that if I am afraid to work in a prison, I should look for another job. Like some teachers who work in

our school system. If teachers do not respect and inspire their students because they are afraid of them, they should not be in classrooms. My personality is one that makes inmates comfortable. I am a firm, no-nonsense, fair counselor, and I love the work I do, which is conveyed to inmates. Many female staff remind residents and inmates of their mothers, sisters, girlfriends, wives, aunts, cousin, etc. So, there is a level of respect. However, there will be inmates who will try you. This chapter focuses on administration and employees' tactics toward residents or inmates. Most staff are positive, however, there are some who are not. I noticed how residents and inmates were spoken to by staff. Some did not respect residents. Nighttime was worse for residents. I witnessed some staff cursing and verbally disrespecting residents, when I complained about this behavior towards residents, their attitude implied "I was taking the resident or inmate's side," which was totally false. I explained to the staff that residents or inmates should be spoken to and treated with respect as they wanted to be treated and I was not taking anyone's side. To staff reading this book, I know the type of people we are dealing with, I also know that all should be respected. There were some residents who had not been home for years. There were some residents who had not seen the outside world for close to fifteen years. I was a new counselor, working in the prison system, this was alarming to me. I remember an incident when I sent a resident to a local employment center for job search. He was a Caucasian brother from the southern part of NJ. I asked him to come to the office so I could see how he was dressed. He came to the office appropriately dressed; I issued him a pass to go to the One Stop Employment Center. He returned that afternoon and stopped by my office. I asked him how it went.

"Ms. Bey, this is the second time I have been outside".

"Really?" I replied.

"Yes, the first time was when I was locked up fifteen years ago and today when you sent me out for job searching."

"Oh my God, I didn't know. How was it?" I asked him. "It had to be some experience. Was it scary?"

"Ms. Bey, yeah, my problem was dealing with the traffic. When I went to jail fifteen years ago, there was no traffic and the cars looked different too, as a matter of fact everything is different."

We both laughed.

"That was an experience Ms. Bey. I don't think I am going to make it."

"Why would you say that?" I asked him.

"Everything is so different, Ms. Bey. I am not prepared for this. It reminds me of *The Shawshank Redemption* movie. You know, when the old man went home after being in jail for more than fifty years? That life was all he knew, and when they released him, he went to a rooming house, got himself a job as a grocery boy. He was miserable. He feared the traffic, like I did today. Everything he knew was in the prison. Well, if you saw that movie Ms. Bey, you know he hung himself. And I understand why he would do that. Ms. Bey, I don't think I can make it."

I assured him he would make it. I reminded him that the Brook's character in the movie was an institutionalized old man. I reminded him that he was a young man with potential. I asked him if I could be candid with him.

"Yes, Ms. Bey, I know you want me to succeed."

"Here's the deal," I said. "Being afraid of traffic is normal. You were afraid of the traffic because your weight makes it difficult for you to run and because of other things you have mentioned to me. But you have some good things going for you."

"Like what?" he asked me.

"You acquired your high school diploma, you worked in the kitchen, so you have culinary skills. You are young, have the right attitude. You will be with me for approximately four months. I will make a medical appointment for you to get a physical examination. You will come to my office weekly, so we can discuss plans for your release. I want you to think about your goals. Write it out and give it to me by the end of the week. Now trust me, when you begin to see a difference in your weight and you start to get your energy back, you will notice a significant change in your attitude about going outside. You think you can do that for me?" I asked him.

"You got it Ms. Bey. No one has ever done this for me Ms. Bey, thank you."

He started to cry. He was a broken spirit. I said to him, "You are going to be just fine and stop thinking about that movie." He laughed and left my office. Now I could have had the attitude, that he was just another inmate, why should I care about him? I make no exceptions with the brothers and sisters I work(ed) with. Everyone, Black, White, Latino, male, female, receives the same counseling they need from me to change their lives. All of them are "broken." The ironic thing about the corrections system is that it does not correct behavior. I don't know why it is called the corrections system. As the resident stated, he was not prepared for the outside world. In my experience, inmates who have been incarcerated for years and are released to halfway houses have not been rehabilitated or equipped for the outside world. By releasing such individuals back into society, the system is not taking into consideration that these men and women have been locked up and away from society for years without any reintegration or preparation for life in society. Reentry begins inside, prior to their release. Meaning if they do not have their high school diploma or GED, get it while they are incarcerated. They should be prepared to work by receiving training or credentials prior to their release. The system expects halfway house staff, and organizations to train residents for release back into society in six months, regardless of the time they have spent in prison, this is unrealistic—particularly if they have been locked up for years. It is a process they must go through. However, if programs or lectures does not focus on the needs of inmates while they are incarcerated, we are wasting taxpayer's dollars. Once inmates are released back into society, they must have skills that allows them to obtain employment. Prisons should offer construction trades, Commercial Drivers Licenses (CDL), culinary arts, job readiness skills, mental health and attitude adjustment classes this requirement will support inmates in obtaining employment, allowing them to be productive responsible citizens rather than returning to a life of crime. Programming, lectures, groups, and caseload meetings must be geared toward inmates' rehabilitation and preparation for the outside world. However, if there are some counselors or staff degrading inmates, disrespecting them or have low expectations of them to achieve their goals as it happens in our schools. Once they are released from prison, halfway house, or jail, it is no wonder many ex-offenders return to prison, going back to what they know which is criminal activity. Students who are miseducated or not inspired or academically challenged, drop out of school, creating a path of criminal activity on their way to prison. Prisoners are viewed by society as dangerous and many are—but many other are not. Some taxpayers believe that locking up people will solve the problem of crime; they do not understand the need for prisoners to be rehabilitated or receive training while they are behind the walls. However, when a family member becomes an inmate, this is when they want their loved ones to take advantage of education and training, anger management, mental health support, Alcohol Anonymous (AA) and Narcotics Anonymous

(NA) while they are incarcerated. Taxpayers must understand prisoners will return home to their communities. The concern should be, "What type of person they want returning home?" The type of individual returning home to our communities depends on the quality of programs and training and mental health services offered while incarcerated. I have to continue repeating preparing prisoners for reentry back into society begins inside the prisons before their release. As taxpayers, we are not saving money if we do not prepare inmates for their return to society as well as educate and train staff in this area. Which will support inmates to become responsible citizen when released. Small example. When an individual enters prison as a high school dropout at least they should obtain their GED while they are imprisoned. There was an emergency staff meeting held by upper management. The agenda was losing residents and the cost involved. Their solution was sanctioning inmates to keep them in the program longer, which would generate more funds. This meant if residents disrespected the staff, did not follow rules, got out of line, did not fix their beds, complained about conditions of facilities or if staff disrespected them or if the resident disagreed with any staff, it could mean they would be sent back to prison. Since inmates did not want to go back to prison, and of course staff who held those conditions over the inmates knew that as well, this behavior was punitive to inmates. I was surprised with this approach in our staff meeting. I commented in this staff meeting that I could not understand why losing residents would be an issue since there will always be criminals. I was a new staff member with new lens, I was becoming acquainted with the prison system. The staff's concern was if we prepared residents, we would not have enough funds to operate the program. I totally disagreed. I remarked, I thought it was our responsibility to prepare inmates by changing their criminal thinking and attitude. I reminded the staff there are many inmates who want to change their lives and realize the need to have qualified staff to assist them, which is why as counselors we are valuable to them. Some staff view at their jobs as a source of income, which it is, rather than an opportunity to change lives of those inmates they are in charge of. Once inmates are released back into society, many of them are scared, and afraid to admit it. We must help these men and women prior to their release. In doing so we will change their mind-set and how they perceive themselves. Inmates have different needs. However, they all must: 1) learn how to manage their mind, 2) understand why they exist, 3) know their goals in life, 4) know their purpose, and 5) be respectful. These qualities will help them see the importance of education, obtain skills, positive attitude, and responsibility. Inmates will self-medicate or relapse because they cannot endure the pressures of life, they become stressful due to their not being able to navigate life. They will revert to their old habits of drinking or drugging or their choice of addictions. Furthermore, many inmates and residents have burned their bridges with relatives due to their criminal lifestyle. Family members are sick and tired of their drama and do not want it brought back to their homes. Residents not only have employment, educational, or attitude issues, they have housing and health issues too. Being stuck in situations such as these contributes to their anger issues. They blame everyone for their condition rather than examining themselves and taking responsibility for their actions. The power of counselors is significant to residents', student's growth, and their development. If there are staff who do not believe in them, correcting the inmate's criminal thinking or a student's perception of their ability to academically succeed will prove problematic. Besides, we must look at residents returning to the neighborhoods they left. They are met with the same issues—new faces, same game. Current programming, groups, and lectures do not relate to inmates who are mainly Black and Hispanic. It's similar to the educational system. The educational system's curriculum does not focus on black children with respect to their history. We must design a curriculum that is conducive to all students regardless of their color. The history and contributions of black people are not discussed in schoolbooks, which makes a difference in the development of black children. This is just as critical in the prison system, where programs that are used are not directly relevant to inmates. The curriculum does not have valid subjects for inmates to relate to. Some counselors teaching these groups do not understand the backgrounds of inmates nor where they come from. Presentation is essential. I am not saying all counselors are incompetent. But they must be innovative as well as creative, interesting and engaging. There are great counselors. However, how to educate and train inmates requires experience, maturity, and skill. I recall an inmate expressing to me. "Ms. Bey, I am fifty-two years old, what can a twenty-five-year-old tell me about life"? There are too many young counselors. Young counselors are well-meaning; however, they must have ongoing training. Hiring young counselors may save money for these institutions but this decision does not invest in inmates. The younger counselor is not experienced enough to give critical advice to older inmates. Not only does the information have to be relevant to the resident, but also the person(s) who is speaking to residents. If the presentation by the speaker is mundane, dull, or lacking in related information, the inmate will feel as our children do in schools when they are being miseducated. As a matter of fact, in the prisons there is a saying: "**You feel me**?" Meaning, inspire them to want to change their lives. You must "feel them". There are some staff who will use their employee badges and positions as a weapon to control inmates. My oldest son was in federal prison for five years; he was later released to a halfway house in Newark, NJ. My daughter contacted me to let me know what was going on with him because he would not tell me. My attitude was he made his bed; he must lay in it. However, once she informed me the counselor threatened to send him back to prison and was using her status as a counselor to intimidate him became a different concern for me. Within a week he was written up for being disrespectful because he requested a pass to go on a job interview. It was and is a condition for an inmate's release to find employment; you would think some counselors would be more accommodating and assist inmates by providing opportunities for them to get employment. Nope. My son's counselor was unprofessional with a negative attitude. She told him if he continued to request a pass, she would send him back to prison. As a counselor, I have never threatened an inmate with sending them back to prison unless there were verbal or physical threats. Other than that, the inmate's behavior would be addressed according to their behavior displayed. I contacted the Director in charge of that facility to let him know what this counselor was doing to my oldest son. The Director contacted the counselor. My son was allowed to get his pass to fill out job applications. However, the counselor did not like what occurred and eventually, he was sent back to prison. Why would a person use their position over an inmate? Answer: Power. I know that if that same staff member met a former inmate on the outside, their attitude would be different. There is no way that staff would bully or be disrespectful, which is probably why many staff do not live in Newark, because they will encounter former inmates or residents upon their release. I know because I see them on a regular basis since I do live in Newark. We must change tactics used towards inmates if we want to see a positive change in their behavior which will result in better communities. As we know, attitude is everything. If we do not adjust our strategies and techniques in staff development inside prisons, halfway houses and schools, we will continue to create "broken spirits."

STAFF CAN BE BROKEN SPIRITS TOO

Halfway houses and treatment facilities hire former residents or inmates. The founder of this facility and a former inmate himself felt formerly incarnated individuals should be given a second chance. He experienced firsthand how difficult it is for residents to acquire employment with a criminal record, (this is compounded if you are black or Hispanic). The staff were innovative in creating programs, motivating groups, and giving lectures that transformed inmates. Statistics show that if you have staff who are genuinely concerned about the positive outcome of residents, these programs will be a substantial success for inmates, the facility, and the community. However, as with any company, organization, or business, some employees bring their baggage of unresolved issues to work. Write-ups were one of the main issues. This behavior clashed with staff who were never incarcerated. Some previous residents who were staff did not see a problem with residents caught smoking. There were some of us who perceived this as a problem since changing behavior and following rules were critical to a resident's success and progress. I understood and appreciated the founder opening these facilities to help formerly incarcerated men and women obtain employment. Those of us with family or friends who have felonies know that it is difficult for them to find employment. Today there are companies and organizations that recognize formerly incarcerated individuals are hard workers and want to be given a second chance. The requirements for former residents to work in these facilities include a) have not committed any new offences within eighteen months, b) availability of additional credentials c) possession of a driver's licenses d) having GEDs and/or a high school diploma. We are warehousing inmates if we are not creating strategies to transform residents while they are incarcerated, no matter how much time they are serving. Changing behavior is part of developing character and a positive attitude. There are many people who came to prison and found their purpose because they used their time wisely to develop their talents and the courage to discover their gifts.

Jamal Joseph, one of the Panther 21. In the late sixties, Jamal served time in Rikers Island and was charged with conspiracy as one of the Panther 21. He landed back in prison serving twelve years at Leavenworth, where he earned two degrees. He is now a professor at the film division of Columbia University School of Arts, the very school he encouraged students to burn down during one of his speeches as a Panther. He is the author of "Panther Baby."

Jeff Henderson, at twenty-one years old, was making $35,000 a week as one of the top cocaine dealers in San Diego, CA. At the age of twenty-three, he was sentenced to twenty years for drug trafficking. He began cooking in prison and it was here that he found his purpose as a chef. Upon his release, he was hired at Café Bellagio in Las Vegas as the executive chef. Today he is lovingly referred to as Chef Jeff. He has a TV show and a training program that helps formerly incarcerated young people who are interested in the culinary field. Chef Jeff is the author of *Cooked: From the Streets to the Stove, from Cocaine to Foie Gras*.

Shaka Senghor was in prison for nineteen years for murder during the eighties crack epidemic. Seven of those years were spent in solitary confinement. During this time, he discovered his gifts as a writer, motivational speaker, and mentor. He is the author of *Writing My Wrongs*, which is the story of what came next. He now works with Oprah Winfrey.

As staff, we are given the opportunity to renew residents' minds and support them in believing it's possible to live their dreams, regardless of their circumstance. However, residents or inmates must want to change their behavior. Staff who are "broken spirits" require assistance too. As staff, we tell our clients to ask for help, but we must ask for help too. Most staff who are working in the prison system or have worked in the prison system are professional and respectful to their coworkers. Yet there are those co-workers who are not, this behavior can cause negative effects in counselors' abilities to reinforce and maintain their belief that residents can change their behaviors. If some staff are displaying negative behaviors towards each other, they must know residents are watching. Staff is important in this process. As employees, we must demonstrate positive, respectful examples for inmates and students so that they are confident in their ability to become successful in life. To heal the lives of inmates and students, we must heal ours. I love Charlamagne tha God's new book *Shook One*. In his second book he focuses on mental health. Recognizing we have issues is vital to helping ourselves and others. Below is a preview of his new book. I salute Charlamagne for his focus on mental health. Charlamagne tha God—*New York Times'* bestselling author of *Black Privilege* and provocative cohost of Power 105.1 FM's The Breakfast Club—revealed his blueprint for breaking free from fears and anxieties. Charlamagne found himself still being paralyzed by anxiety and distrust. Now, in *Shook One*, he is working through these problems—many of which he traces back to cultural PTSD—with help from mentors, friends, and therapy. Being anxious doesn't serve the same purpose anymore. Through therapy, he's figuring out how to get over the irrational fears that won't take him anywhere positive.

GRANDMOTHER WHO DEMANDED
GRANDSON SELL DRUGS

I know it is difficult for many of us financially, and in some cases, we don't know how we are going to make it and at times we all do crazy things because we just do not think. I am sure many of you can relate to this. When you are going through something that is or can be traumatic, you may not see a way out and do what comes naturally. You don't realize how you got yourself into a mess and how you will get out. Many mothers feel the pain of supporting their family—I know I have felt it too. But to ask your son or your grandson to sell drugs rather than attend a basketball camp and school that could take him out of illegal behavior is reprehensible. This young man came into my office, looking distressed. He said he wanted my advice. I asked him to sit down. He was a tall, handsome, nineteen-year-old young man. He had his diploma and was offered a scholarship to a basketball camp in Florida. He was a well-known drug dealer in southern NJ. He said to me he was in a dilemma. He informed me he had two brothers and he lived with his mother and grandmother. He wanted my advice regarding a decision he had to hurry up and make. His grandmother told him that when he came home, she wanted him to sell drugs because he had to take care of the family. He said she was making him feel guilty because he no longer wanted to sell drugs. I asked him what was his mother's position? He said, she wanted him to sell drugs too.

"Even if it meant you could get killed in the process?" I asked.

He did not respond. I asked him, if there was something else. He said yes. He stated he was accepted to a basketball camp in Florida. He wanted to go there, but he also wanted to take care of his brothers, and if he did not sell drugs and go to basketball camp instead, he would feel guilty because he felt responsible for his brothers. You cannot make this stuff up. I was appalled. I could not respond right away because this young man was visibly distressed. It was obvious he wanted to go to Florida. I asked him a couple more questions. Then I gave him my answer. I assured him that he was not responsible for his brothers though he loves them—as he should. However, he was not their father or provider. I told him that it was shameful his mother and grandmother would make such a request and making him feel guilty in the process. I told him his mother and grandmother should be ashamed of themselves. We discussed this for some time; it was important he knew it was not his responsibility. I expressed to him that if he was my son, I would want him to take advantage of the basketball camp. This was an opportunity to be drafted in the NBA, though they knew he had been a drug dealer. I convinced him he was getting a second chance, and that in the long run, if he wanted to provide for his family, he could do it legally and would not have to worry about looking over his shoulder. I emphasized to him that the responsibility of taking care of his family was not his, but that of his mother and grandmother. I asked permission to call his mother and grandmother, he declined, he would not allow me to contact them. Reaching this decision was painful for him. However, he did feel comfortable expressing his concerns to me which allowed him to make the best decision for himself. Having someone to confide in allowed him to talk through his pain. The decision was his to make. Therefore <u>concerned, skilled counselors and teachers are key</u> to the decision-making process for inmates, particularly since they have made bad decisions in the past. I wish I could report a positive outcome. Unfortunately, I do not know the conclusion of his decision. He was released shortly thereafter. I hope he went to Florida. I must continue to emphasize the importance of experienced and capable counselors and how important they are to inmates and students. Those of you who are **counselors** or **teachers** I want you to realize

how vital you are to inmates and students. As an empathetic counselor or teacher, we know that we can inspire many "broken spirits" by what we say and how we say it to them. As with any career, you have to love what you do. When I worked behind the walls, I looked forward to going to work. I was excited about getting busy helping brothers and sisters. When I lectured, I expected interactive and intelligent discussions by residents, not arguments. I prepared lectures as though I was teaching in college. I had high expectations of inmates to receive the message delivered to them. Most effective counselors and teachers know, we do make a difference in inmates and students' lives. By instilling confidence, trust and bolstering their self-esteem is significant to their success. That is why I believe it is imperative when brothers and sisters are released from prison, they continue their mental health counseling and are assigned a mentor, like Alcoholics Anonymous or Narcotics Anonymous.

GANG RIVALRY AT DELANEY HALL

We had a situation, like all treatment facilities and prisons do. In this case, it was regarding gang members who were rivaling against each other. The gang leader in question was a high-ranking gang member on my caseload. I did not know at the time he was a gang member. However, he came to me to let me know what was going on with him.

"Okay," I said, "What is it you want me to do?"

He told me he would have to be moved because he did not want no trouble and he did not want his pups to get hurt. I asked him what his dogs have to do with this. He said, "No Ms.

Bey, not my dogs, my little homies—they have to protect me, and I don't want anything to happen to them." He pointed to a group of young men who seemed to be in their twenties outside my office, "I'm off this shit," he said. We went to the Director of Operations to let him know what was going on. I asked the resident to sit outside the office, so I could speak to the director. The director said he would move him off the tier into another location in the building. He instructed me to take him back to his room to get his belongings. As we were gathering his things, the resident told me a group of brothers were coming to the room to off him (kill). My back was turned, so I could not see them. I asked him to let me know as they got closer. When he did, I turned around, looked at them and said hi, I felt no fear. They did nothing and stayed outside the room. However, the gang leader whispered to me, "Ms. Bey, they want to do it now."

"Those brothers?"

"Yes."

"Okay," I said, "I will stay with you until we get you downstairs."

As we were walking out of the room, I asked the brothers if everything was alright. They said, "Yes, Ms. Bey." Okay, I responded, "I will speak to you brothers when I come back upstairs."

Now if these brothers could have easily knocked me down to get to this brother. The reason they did not was they respected me.

When we got downstairs to Operations, I informed the director what just happened. Because the gang leader's safety was at risk, the director transferred him to another location out of the building. As most counselors know, we must document all incidents. The director called me to his office to discuss the incident. He asked me why I did not know this resident was a high-ranking gang member. That question reminded me of my first encounter with J, the gang member at Kintock. My response to the director was the same as it was to the previous director.

"I don't ask them if they are gang members."

He asked me if during intake did, I ask the resident if he was a gang member.

"No, I did not," I replied.

"Why?" the director asked.

"I don't because I am assuming all residents are gang members. I am their counselor. I help them to think about the things they have done, to have remorse for what they have done. As their counselor I focus on the behaviors that caused them to become incarcerated. It is clear he felt comfortable approaching me to let me know about the issue. I am not here to judge them, but to correct their behavior and their criminal thinking."

"Have the Incident Report on my desk before you leave today, Ms. Bey," he stated.

"Yes sir," I replied.

NOTE: As Counselors and Teachers, we do save lives. I am sure there are many counselors who can tell other stories like this and can appreciate what I am sharing. There must be trust on the part of the resident to share with us their concerns, their dreams, their pain, and their hurts. Changing criminal thinking and addictive behaviors takes time and understanding. Many counselors understand what I am talking about.

FAHEEM SHABAZZ, FROM THE BASEMENT TO REAL ESTATE, CONSTRUCTION and INVESTMENT

I met Faheem Shabazz 2013 through a friend who shared with me Faheem's story. I invited Faheem to Delaney Hall to speak with residents about his story. He shared with residents how he came from living in his mother's basement to real estate investor, construction management and investment companies. He informed residents that after 10 ½ years in prison the US Supreme Court overturned his case, he gained his freedom March 11th, 1997. He was no longer a DOC number (department of corrections). He was no longer told to squat and bend over by guards. He was no longer on the count. He told the residents when he was released from prison, he was also released from a criminal thinking mindset because of the mentoring he received by older inmates in prison. Faheem became a strong determined motivated individual who gave back to his community by training, hiring, and housing formerly incarcerated returning citizens. He was committed in making a positive transformation for these individuals because he came from their lifestyle. Faheem came from the ghettos of America, involved in the drug life of America served time in the prisons of America and changed his life to one of unrecognizable. The new Faheem Shabazz was successful, happy, positive, caring, spiritual being who appreciated life. He realized sharing his knowledge about his experiences was helpful and a positive impact on young men and women who believed the streets were their only option to be successful. Faheem proved them wrong. He showed them options through hard work and consistency.

He talked about his Prison Reform Ministry and why he traveled across the country speaking to prisoners to encourage them to do the right thing once they were released and if they needed help to call him. He mentioned he sent money to inmates to put on their commissaries because he wanted to give back to them because they helped him when he was inside. He told how many of his friends inside the prison did not have family but to him they were his family. He wrote letters to them about what was happening on the outside and what he would do for them once they were released. They looked forward to his letters and packages.

I observed residents/inmates when Faheem came with me in halfway houses and prisons. They loved him and was always happy to see him. Many of them knew him because they were doing what he used to do, which was sold drugs. His success motivated residents/inmates to aspire to be productive in their lives and change their criminal lifestyle. He became a regular speaker at Delaney Hall. He told about his dream to buy his mother a house and when he did the feeling was exhilarating. He traveled to Florida on a regular basis to see his mom. Faheem emphasized to residents the importance of taking care of their children and to be a positive role model and to think about their legacy, what do they want to be remembered for and what are they leave their families. He told them he made sure he was available for his children and on Saturdays he took his children to Barnes and Nobles Book store and cooked dinner for his family. He was in heaven.

Once I saw the value Faheem brought to this population, I asked him to come with me when I go into the prisons. We formed a friendship that was supportive of each other. He was supportive of me and in my community activities. He was a 4 Hour of Power Honoree in 2018 and received a resolution from The City of Newark 2019 recognizing him for his participation in The Delaney Hall Day. He appeared on my tv show Tell a Vision when it first aired in 2016. He became a regular guest.

When I published my first book, Broken Spirit, Let It Go So You Can Grow. He was supportive. He purchased my books and sent them to prisons. I thanked him for his support. He was incredibly happy for me he said "Ms. Bey, you care, you ain't like those people". We would laugh when I responded.

"you got that right; I don't want to be like them". Unfortunately, I lost my friend to The Corona Virus February 2021. He will always be in my heart and the brothers and sisters who knew him. Faheem Shabazz encouraged young people and activated their Greatness. He helped them understand the answers they are seeking are within and they are responsible for their own success. Rest in Peace, Bro. Shabazz. Job well done.

LANCE MCGRAW FROM
FROM INMATE TO VICTORY

Lance McGraw a young man whose story is one of triumph and amazement. I met Lance McGraw in 2018. Lance was employed with a local reentry program that the City of Newark partnered with. At the time I was the Newark Reentry Manager. Lance was a Job Coach for this local reentry program. His presentations and workshops for Returning Citizens or formerly incarcerated individuals for this reentry program were powerful, comprehensive, inspirational as well as professional. Observing his interaction with clients during lectures, I recognized his passion. However, I did not know at the time he had another gift. Lance perfected his talent in training by developing "HUSTLEUTION" trainings. His training consisted of individuals who inspired Lance in personal development while he was in prison. One of Lance's quotes from HUSTLEUTION "You can always replace the position, but you can't replace the PERSON".

Two of Lance's favorite quotes by Jim Rohn, are. "Don't wish it were easier, wish you were better", "Don't wish for less problems, wish for more skills". Lance took personal development seriously while he was incarcerated and learned to use and apply his skills. Those of us who work as job coaches, counselors, case managers, know it is about personal development and responsibility. As I got to know Lance, another passion I discovered of his was cooking with his business partner. Together the dynamic duo created LYRICAL

CHEF. So, between working at the reentry program, Lance was polishing his trainings and honing his culinary skills. That is a hustler. 2 or 3 jobs at a time. You know, multitask. As much as Lance loved his job with this reentry program, God had something epic waiting for him. Individuals like Lance working at these programs are never paid their worth for the value they bring to these programs, nor are they given the opportunity to use their gifts to help others. Many become "haters" and are intimidated by your shine. I know. We all experienced this. Here is the key, no matter what they do, keep hustling because your hustle is bringing you to your purpose as it did with Lance.

One day as we were talking and Lance casually said he was a 50 Cent fan, I smiled cause y'all who read Broken Spirit Let It Go So You Can Grow know I am a 50 Cent fan too and that has not changed (LOL). I invited Lance to join me on a few occasions when I spoke at various churches and organizations. We conducted a Parent Reentry Training class at The Newark Public Schools Parent Conference. We also created the first Delaney Hall Reentry Services Project for the City of Newark. It was so successful, the GEO Group, a National Reentry organization highlighted our project in their national newsletter. Lance received a proclamation from the City of Newark for his participation in the project. He has appeared several times on my tv show Tell a Vision and in 2019 he was one of the honorees for 4 Hours a Power. Lance was terminated from this local reentry program 2020 during the Covid 19 Pandemic. Fortunately, while working at the local reentry program, Lance saw the writing on the wall. He was conducting meetings with executives from ShopRite, a major cooperative of supermarkets with stores in six states. After Lance's presentation, ShopRite Management was impressed and took a chance on Lance the window of opportunities unfolded for Lance. God had something greater for him. Today, Lyrical Chef makes the best banana pudding and deserts in the state, as my son says', "it's official". Lance hires formerly incarcerated men and women. He began with 8 Shop Rites and will soon be expanding to 52 more sites, WOW, that is powerful! He purchased a warehouse to accommodate his flourishing company. Lance is "Moving on Up"! There is no stopping, Lance McGraw. An inspiration to all young people whether they have been imprisoned or not. But for those who have been in prison, Lance is proving professional development is an investment in YOU. The willingness to put the work in your hustle pays off. Just ask Lance.

Lance McGraw was born and raised in Newark, NJ. Lance's Father was a drug addict and eventually succumbed to AIDS. To help support his mother who was a victim of domestic violence, at nine years old young Lance provided for his family, by washing car windows. He made $25 a day, gave $20 to his mother for food and kept $5 for himself. Lance became involved in the drug game at fourteen years old. He left the streets at twenty years old. He went back to school, earned his G.E.D. He married and eventually secured his dream job working on Wall Street. Lance suffered a nervous breakdown. As a result, he lost his dream job. Divorced, depressed and unemployed, Lance found himself back in the projects selling drugs, a life he thought he left behind ten years ago.

Lance served a five-year prison sentenced for selling drugs. While serving his time. Lance began reading self-improvement books that gave him a new mindset and surrounded himself with prisoners who were also on the trajectory of positive change. Immediately upon his release, Lance vowed to himself he would become the man he was destined to be. With hard work, consistency and patience, Lance graduated from inmate to motivational speaker, and a job coach. Lance is the founder and leader of the movement HUSTLEUTION (The evolution of a hustler)! Lance continues to devote his life to assist, educate and empower those brothers and sisters returning home from prison so they do not make the same mistakes he did.

Lance had many setbacks. At some point in our lives, we become a broken spirit. However, his experiences helped him to be the man he was becoming, he speaks truth to power. He is an example, as Les Brown, national motivational speaker says, "if you can look up, you can get up". Lance is a loving father and places emphasis on family. Lance made no excuses, took responsibility for his actions and today, he is a living example, of a person who is no longer the problem in his community, but rather, the solution.

TONY OLAJUWON – THE COACH

I met Tony February 2002 when I worked as the Legislative Aide to Councilwoman At-Large Bessie Walker. He was referred to our office by Mayor Sharpe James office. I brought him in the office and introduced myself. Tony had a big smile with beautiful teeth and a great attitude. He was a serious gentleman man who also had a sense of humor. Tony was dressed appropriately for an interview. He disclosed to me he was recently released from prison after serving approximately seventeen years for kidnap and armed robbery. He said to me he needed a job. He worked in the kitchen and maintenance while he was in prison. Once I received all his information. I informed him I would give it to the councilwoman.

Tony informed me he was homeless and living in a shelter. He did not want to go back to prison. Though I was just meeting him for the first time, I knew he was serious. But he told me something that concerned me. He was offered several bricks (drugs) to sell. I realized he was in a vulnerable, desperate situation. I mentioned that he could not do that because he had too much to offer. I did not want to see him return to prison. I assured him the councilwoman would contact him and not to do anything stupid like sell those drugs. Fortunately, he did not.

When he left, I called the councilwoman to inform her of Tony. She asked me to make an appointment for him to meet with her. They met the next day. When he came to the office, I asked Tony to have a seat while I speak to the councilwoman. I brought Tony in the councilwoman's office, she asked him more questions to get clarification of his convictions. She hired him as an Aide. Tony proved to be beneficial to the office, particularly for brothers and sisters coming home from prison or jail. Newark residents released from prison always found their way to Councilwoman Walker's office. Tony was always willing to do what was needed in the office, he worked well with staff. He was aware of the needs of those returning home as a matter of fact he brought them to the office. Those who are serious in changing their lives when they come home from prison, he will refer them to me. While Tony was in prison, he was athletic. When Tony was hired by the Councilwoman, we talked a lot about his charges, his regrets and his dreams. Though he made mistakes when he was a teenager Tony was intelligent and wanted to make up for his past mistakes. I suggested he consider working with youth after school.

Tony saved his money while he was in the shelter in two months, he rented a small apartment, we were all happy for him. Tony felt he was now in a better position to be involved in his daughter's life since he had been out of her life for many years. He wanted to reconnect with her, win her trust. He accomplished all that by visiting her at her home, going to her school to check on her progress, he came to work every day and one day he brought his daughter to work and introduced her to us. I noticed the more Tony became involved in the community he was building momentum for his purpose. Tony started working with gang members to assist them in bringing stability in their lives. Working in a community conscious councilwoman's office provides many opportunities. Tony began taking advantage of those opportunities.

Councilwoman Walker supported him in his community efforts. Tony was a member of the Street Warriors, brothers who served time in prison and decided to improve the quality of life in our communities. I wanted to include Tony in Broken Spirit let it go so you can grow because when I met Tony he was broken. Though his mental attitude was excellent, he was determined to make a difference in the lives of young men. He was given an opportunity to change his life by Councilwoman Walker, he wanted to provide opportunities to the young men he was coaching. He was given the title "the coach".

Today, Tony continues to work with youth. He is involved in his daughter's life, he is a loving, supported father. He speaks at schools, faith-based institutes, universities, colleges, prisons and youth detention center. Tony Olajuwon went to prison a young man came out years later with a new attitude. Tony a man transformed who speaks raw truth. He embraced his passion discovered his purpose and stepped into his power by empowering young people. Tony has received many awards for his involvement in uplifting our community. 2002 I met a Broken Spirit who let it go so he could grow. Tony is the President and Founder of "Constant Justice for Youth Change, LLC. His motto is "Education is a process, which no man or woman can be robbed". Tony blossomed into a spirit of accomplishment by using his skills to transform the lives of young people. In doing so, he became a testimony of success. He ain't no joke.

CHRIS STOKES: NEWARK BOY WAS ONE PERSON HE COULDN'T HUSTLE

Updated Feb 23, 2016; Posted Feb 23, 2016

Christopher Stokes, better known as "Hustleman," said a 7-year-old Newark boy started him on his path of redemption from drugs and crime. He shares his story at Delaney Hall, the place that helped him reclaim his life. The

Newark facility is an alternative to incarceration, a dormitory style home for men who are rebuilding their lives. "Hustleman" remembers July 29, 2012 better than any of the phony aliases, Social Security numbers, or numerous dates of births he used to conceal his identity from authorities. On that day, however, Hustleman met his match. He was 50 years old and couldn't weasel away from a curious 7-year-old <u>Newark</u> boy with a jarring question. "Hustleman, why do you smoke crack?" What bothered him most was that he had no answer as they talked in the hallway of an apartment building at Hyatt Court. It's a Newark public housing development, in which the boy named Samir lived and where the homeless Hustleman slept in a hallway. Hustleman was so quiet that day, you probably could have heard a mosquito doing you-know-what on cotton. "He kept asking me," Hustleman said. "I couldn't answer him." Neither could Christopher Stokes. That's Hustleman's real name. The truth, from a wise little boy, shook him from the grave in which he had lived for 23 years.

Delaney Hall

Stokes is above ground now and he shares that "come to Jesus" moment at Delaney Hall, the place where his ascent back to life took shape. The Newark facility is an alternative to incarceration, a dormitory-style home for men rebuilding lives they maimed with <u>crime and addiction</u>. Once a week for the past two years, Stokes has returned to Delaney to deliver a message that is blunt and raw, and one its residents need to hear. "Only a fool refuses knowledge," he said. "I was tired of being a fool." The majority of the men listen, their eyes fixed on Stokes as he walks up and down the aisle of a large room. Stokes tells them that he stopped running four years ago and turned himself in to the police. He was wanted for several burglaries—crimes he had committed to feed his addiction. The men can relate. Hustleman's dead-end story was the same as theirs, and he has a scorecard as proof: Fifty-three drug arrests and two prison terms totaling 18 months; four felonies; eight trips to Delaney Hall; and the possibility of a five-year jail sentence. None of it fazed Hustleman, he told the group. "I got comfortable going to jail." he said. He weighed 112 pounds and had only three teeth. They were so crooked, Stokes jokes that his homies in the room said it looked like they were throwing up gang signs. The men crack up. He's a funny guy, but he's serious, too, telling them that they can no longer make excuses.

The Comeback

That was his approach after his charges were reduced and he was allowed to enroll in a drug court program. Lessons from Delaney Hall began to make sense. He didn't slump in his seat during sessions as some of the men were doing as he talked to them. Stokes isn't offended, because the men paying attention come to him for insight. His journey back, he said, unfolded with some "emotional deep-sea diving," so he could love himself again. "You've got to do that moral inventory of yourself," he said. When he did, good things started to happen. After he left Delaney Hall in 2013, Stokes reconnected with Maryam Bey, a former caseworker at the facility. She had moved onto Newark's re-entry program, but told him to look her up for training, employment and services. Stokes didn't play. He now weighs 190 pounds and shows off a new set of pearly white teeth. "I was going to be on interviews. I couldn't be talking to nobody with three teeth and my breath stinking." The men laugh again, but Stokes stays focused on his comeback. He washed dishes. He learned the culinary arts and how to drive a forklift. He found an apartment and recently was hired as a food prep worker at Montclair State University. Bey is proud of him. She saw something in him at Delaney Hall, and encouraged him to speak at the facility and the Essex County Jail. "It's beautiful for them (men) to hear from someone who has gone through what they've gone through," Bey said. It works, because they've seen the change, even when it seemed unlikely. "If he can do it, then I can do it," said Zikee Thompson, 25. Thompson grew up at Hyatt Court and saw "Hustleman" when he was running wild. He remembers Samir, too, and how Hustleman stopped other kids from bullying him. But at Delaney Hall, Stokes represents the hope that many of the men have lost. "It's like watching my superhero doing his thing," said Quran Johnson, 45. Delaney Hall staff members love to see Stokes. He bounces through halls, sticking his head in and out of offices, making them smile with his motto: "What it is, what it's gonna be and how we gonna do it." Stokes still thinks about Samir, who moved away from Hyatt Court. It's been two years since he's seen the boy, but Stokes would like to thank him again if he gets the chance. You were compassionate, Samir, when Hustleman couldn't answer your question. You hugged him and told him that everything was going to be all right. You said he was "a good dude" who had a "good heart." Samir, you made Hustleman understand that you were the vessel to help Christopher Stokes get to where he stands today. **Barry Carter**: (973) 836-4925 or bcarter@starledger or nj.com/carter or follow him on Twitter @BarryCarterSL

SISTERS INCARCERATED

The fastest-growing prison population are women. Women who are incarcerated are quite different from men. As women we have many issues—not to minimize the struggles

their way to finding themselves. We must not judge them. To help them and all of us understand if they (we) do not feel good about themselves (ourselves), they will not be able to help their families. We must get women to think about themselves and their value. It is crucial sisters and brothers begin to look at themselves, stop making excuses, begin to live responsibly and with a purpose. As we know, when we make excuses, we do not hold ourselves responsible for our actions Sometimes as many of us know, facing ourselves can be scary because we fear reliving the pain, which is why many brothers and sisters are in prison for drug or alcohol addictions—they are afraid they want to avoid the pain associated with telling their stories. It is a blessing as counselors we can assist sisters to face their fears and help them understand their worth! Counseling is a needed resource for sisters once they are released, partly due to the fact they have issues that have not been addressed. The key is doing something about it, and as counselors and teachers, I personally believe, it is our responsibility to guide them.

Prisoners have no rights, as a matter of fact, the United States Constitution, 13th Amendment states

"Neither slavery nor involuntary servitude, except as a punishment for crime whereof the party shall have been dully convicted, shall exist within the United States, or any place subject to jurisdiction".

So, when you become an inmate under the constitution you are a slave. Unfortunately, women who have been abused by family members or someone they know, this pattern continues in prisons. As their counselor or case manager, I listened to these women, young and old share their pain and trauma in a group or private counseling. When women enter the prison system, they relive the horrors of their abuse. Rather than get support from the system, they get more pain by those who are paid through our tax dollars to support and protect them. Like their family members or friends who did not support or protect them. This is another Civil Rights issue on abuse.

To support my remarks of patterns of abuse and sexual abuse recently two articles were written on The Edna Mahan Prison for Women in Clinton, NJ (Union County). It is so sad. I thought about how so many women have suffered. As Oprah Winfrey says in The Color Purple, "All my life I had to fight. I had to fight my daddy. I had to fight my uncles. I had to fight my brothers. A girl child ain't safe in a family of men".

Edna Mahan has a history of abusing female inmates. This is the paradigm of American prisons.

2019, as the Reentry Coordinator, I attended a Job Fair at Edna Mahan on behalf of the City of Newark, NJ. I spoke to the women about their dreams and purpose in life. They loved my display of the books and were surprised most of the authors were formerly incarcerated. When they read the packages, I specifically created for them, they were so happy and said no one had done this for them because they are degraded, demeaned by staff they feel are regarded insignificant to staff. They said I inspired them. Black, White, Hispanic, Transgender inmates had nothing good to say about Edna Mahan facility. They wanted to know how to get released from that dreadful place. They shared with me how the conditions and treatment by staff was degrading. Living conditions were nauseating. They were scared. They were not safe. They feared for their lives. If they expressed to the staff their concerns, they were punished.

When the job fair ended, the women asked me to return and thanked me for the packages I prepared for them. Though I was pleased they were motivated, appreciated my words and packages, I left sad and angry that these beautiful women who were somebody's mother, grandmother, sister, daughter, auntie had to live at "that place".

Please read the articles below on Edna Mahan Prison Facility so you can understand how the continuation of breaking and destroying people in these facilities because staff can, this behavior continue to create broken spirits.

31 Guards Suspended at a Women's Prison Plagued by Sexual Violence - The New York Times (nytimes.com)
By Tracey Tully
Published 1/ 28/ 2021.

NJ women's prison Edna Mahan failed to address sex abuse: DOJ (mycentraljersey.com)
Code of silence' at Edna Mahan allowed 'culture of acceptance' of sexual abuse: DOJ.
Mike Deak
Bridgewater Courier News
Published 4/13/2020.

What these correctional officers (male and female) have done to these inmates is reprehensible and, in my opinion, there is no way government officials, or the courts did not know what was happening behind the walls at The Edna Mahan Prison Facility.

As a counselor, I recognized many women had abandonment and trust issues as a result it was difficult to let go of their past hurts. They became stuck in their pain or betrayal because it was what they knew. Each time they expressed to me their experiences they relived their pain, however, for them to heal, they needed to speak their truth. In most cases their trauma occurred when they were children or teenagers. I stressed to them, it was not their fault, they were not in control as I was not in control when I was raped. I gave them examples of women who walked in their shoes and are impressively successful and wealthy. Oprah Winfrey and Maya Angelou were top of that list. We all need examples of success by those who have gone through what we have been through, so we do not make excuses. invite friends to our pity party or become stuck in our pain.

Is the healing process painful? Yes, very painful but necessary for us to discover our worth and value. As children we had no control of what happened to us. As adults, we have choices. We can choose to carry past baggage's and be unhappy or we can let it go so we can grow to live our destiny and use the gifts given to us to help ourselves and others. There is greatness within. When we take personal inventory, we are designing our future. Our experiences will help us to map our life's journey. Which is what I did. I used my voice, my story, and experiences to show women how I overcame my challenges. This helped them understand they can come out of that painful dark place. I had no idea something as horrific and painful as being raped by my father, abandoned by my mother, and taken from my family I would one day empower and encourage men and women to find their greatness. I discovered my purpose working in the prison system by inspiring men and women to look at the beauty and love within. I reminded them to always be grateful because their past prepared them for their greatness and their ability to discover their destiny and within that preparation is the process of forgiving those who hurt them. The "good news" is The Edna Mahan Correctional Facility was closed Monday June 7, 2021, by Governor Phil Murphy. Shut it down finally. Please read this enlightening article about this women's prison. Women's Prison Plagued by Sexual Violence Will Close, Governor Says - The New York Times (nytimes.com).

RESIDENTS LIVE FOR THAT PHONE CALL

Now I understand the need to stay in touch and connected to your family, especially when you are locked up and have no funds to call home. For those of us who have received collect phone calls, you know how expensive they can be (which is why as a counselor I allowed residents to make phone calls to their families). It was not for the resident's sake, but for their families. I remember one mother called me to say thank you because she could not afford to put money in her son's account to make phone calls and she really appreciated he was as able call home and speak to her. She said it was such a relief. Phone calls for residents are important too so they can inform their families of their needs. I gave phone calls on a weekly basis to residents on my caseload. I worked on Saturdays, and new residents always wanted a phone call. I didn't have to give them a call; their attitude had everything to do with them being able to call their families. I recall how far a resident (grown man) will go to get a phone call. Examples:

1) A resident comes into the office stating he needed to make a phone call that it was an emergency (everything is an emergency). I asked what is the emergency? He responded that his son is having seizures and he wants to call home to check up on him. I ask him how he knew his son was having seizures. He says he was talking to his friend at the end of the hall who said he saw the man's girlfriend, and she told him, "My baby is in the hospital."

"Your baby is in the hospital?" I ask. "Well let's call the hospital to find out how your baby is doing."

"Ms. Bey, I have to call my girl to get the number."

"No, you don't, I have the number. I will call."

We called the hospital. I informed him there was no baby listed under the name he gave me.

"Your baby is not in the hospital, is there anything else I can do for you?"

"No," he responds, and walks out the office.

2) A resident comes into the office upset; he tells me his grandmother has died. I asked how he knows this. "My friend who lives on my block told me; he came in last night. Yeah, Ms. Bey, I just need to call home because I want to find out when they are going to have her funeral, because I want to attend, and I want to talk to my family."

Of course, I give him the phone call. But when he gets on the phone, he says nothing about his grandmother. It's all about what's happening on the block. What's going on with his girl. Who got shot; who's in the hospital—nothing about his grandmother?

"Hold it sir, I thought you were calling about your grandmother who died," I said to him.

"Oh, Yeah, my bad, Ms. Bey."

Those were the two popular ones. These experiences taught me just how far some residents would go to get a phone call. Most of the requested phone calls would be for someone who got shot or who was dead. I changed my requirements for their phone call requests. If they wanted a phone call because someone was in the hospital, they would provide me the name of the hospital, and if someone died and they wanted to know about the funeral arrangements, they would give me the name of the funeral parlor, so I could call to confirm. Residents could be very manipulative—you got to love them for trying. At first, they got me a few times, but then I learned their game. They stopped coming to me for bogus phone calls once they knew the questions, I would ask them, and of course they did not want to answer. They eventually learned all they had to do was be honest with me and they would get the call. I remember an incident that was too funny regarding a phone call and how residents remember how you treat them. I was in Irvington, NJ, on a Monday afternoon. I walked to Don's Restaurant. I saw these three brothers walking towards me. I said to myself what's up. They got closer to me and stopped. I spoke to them. One brother said to me, "I know you."

I said "You do? How?"

"You look really familiar," he said.

"Okay," I replied. **Just a note here**. Whenever a brother says they know me, "I look familiar", I know they have been incarcerated and I just wait for them to remember. This brother said, parole officer. I said No. Probation officer. I said No. Attorney.

"No, but you're getting closer." I replied.

Finally, he yelled, "Ms. Bey!"

I smiled and said you're right. He got excited and hugged me. I couldn't stop him. Here's my point about phone calls. He said to his friends. Ms. Bey saved my life.

"I did?"

"Yeah! Because of the phone call you gave me, I was released the same day. I kept my job and my apartment and my kids."

"Wow, that's nice," I said.

"And my n**** she wasn't my counselor because I came on Saturday and my counselor was not in." He was speaking to his "homies."

"I came home because of you Ms. Bey, thank you." He hugged me again.

I said, "You're welcome, and stay out of trouble."

That day showed me how important **PHONE CALLS ARE to RESIDENTS.** You know, I really love my job. These brothers and sisters educated me in ways books could not with hands-on experiences. Particularly on how to deal with all types of people. Counselors are faced with all types of attitudes. But if you are a proficient counselor, you can recognize which character you will be dealing with on a particular day, afternoon, or night. When I began working with this population, I believed everything they told me. I soon realized they were manipulating me. It took me a while to understand that. Now I just laugh. Experience is the best teacher. I am not offended by what they do. You can't get mad; this has been their lifestyle. They are not going to change overnight. They are still "broken spirits." Next, working with inmates gave me the ability to prepare them for another level in their lives. So many of them were "broken spirits" and I realized that a simple word of encouragement uplifted their spirit. The articles I gave them were inspiring, and I worked extremely hard to develop inspirational lectures. I encouraged them to think about the choices they made in their lives, and how they paid for the seats they were sitting in by putting that work in. Why they must take responsibility for their actions. I wanted them to think about their actions that caused them to become a "broken spirit."

OUR CHILDREN CAN BECOME "BROKEN SPIRITS"

Children attending schools can become "Broken Spirits" depending on their teachers and how their teachers view them. Some teachers do not view urban students as worthy or intelligent. Teachers need to be open-minded and nonjudgmental. If teachers do not prepare students for academic excellence, they will prepare them for prison. In many instances this lack of academic preparation, miseducation, or even no education is purposely executed. When my youngest son attended elementary and high school in Newark and my granddaughter attended elementary school in Irvington and Newark, I noticed several things. 1) My granddaughter was treated differently because she was dark-skinned. She is beautiful today and was beautiful when she was a student. However, the impression my granddaughter received from her teachers was that she was not smart. My granddaughter informed me her teachers would always compliment students who were white, or light skinned. This caused my granddaughter to question her worthiness and value due to her teacher(s)' attitude towards the color of her skin rather than the measurement of her intelligence. My granddaughter would cry because of this treatment. This was cruel and malicious punishment by her teachers. Fortunately, she was told how beautiful she was by her mother, family and friends everyday who loved her. Today she is a smart businesswoman. She was encouraged to love her beautiful black skin. Even in 2019, color continues to be an issue. Dark-skinned students are treated differently from their white and light-skinned counterparts. Martin Luther King, Jr's statement "Judge a person by the content of their character and the not the color of their skin" is applicable even today. The power of a teacher's words or expectation of their student to succeed intellectually as well as emotionally definitely has an impact on students' success or failure. 2) I noticed the majority of my son's teachers were women. I observed those female teachers would transfer their problems with their husbands or boyfriends to their male students. Because my son was vocal and expressed his opinions, this caused problems with some of his teachers. I received a call from his principal informing me the school's Child Study Team would like to speak to me regarding my son's behavior. Of course, I was concerned. I came to school to meet with the team. The team informed me they were considering my son for Special Education. But before the decision was made, they would have to visit our home and evaluate my son through academic and emotional tests. Tests regarding his mental health would be administered at the former University of Medicine and Dentistry of New Jersey Behavioral Clinic, which is now operated and owned by Rutgers University. I agreed to his being evaluated, but I made it clear I would not sign any paper unless they proved my son should be placed in special education. After all the evaluations, home visits, etc., I received a call from the social worker saying that the team was ready to make their decision regarding my son, and they would like to meet with me. I made the appointment. I brought my son with me to the meeting. I I wanted him to hear what they would say about him. Once we were brought to the office, I was informed they were recommending my son for special education. I asked why. They said he had a delayed response in solving problems or making decisions, also he did not comprehend classroom assignments as fast as he should. Socially he was not engaging or interacting with his classmates in a constructive manner. My son was ten years old at the time and attending Alexander Street School. I asked them about his evaluation at the Behavioral Clinic. They told me there were no evidence of problems with his brain functions. I was relieved about that. I looked at them and said. I want to be clear on the main reason you are recommending my son for special education. You are stating because my son's reaction is slow, he should be placed in special education, right? They nodded their heads yes. I went on to say,

"Let me explain to you what I am hearing from you about my son." I gave them the following example: "You give my son and his classmates the same problem. His classmates answer the problem before he does, however he does answer the problem. He's just slower, but he gets it."

"Yes," was their response.

"And that's the reason he should be placed in special education?"

"Yes," was their response again. They had papers ready for me to sign. I looked at them and said. "He will attend Vailsburg Middle School. When you informed me The Child Study Team was recommending my son for special education, I visited Vailsburg Middle School's special education class. I stated to the team, my son is not a special education student but if he is placed in special education, he will be. My opinion is you guys dumb down education, give students the perception there is something wrong with them, when there is something wrong with you if you think I am putting my son in special ed. There is nothing wrong with my son, he's ten years old. Every child learns at their own pace. I will not place him in special education. I am not opposed to special education for those students who needs it, my son doesn't. I will not sign any papers. I looked at my son and said, "You see what they think of you? There is nothing wrong with you." I took his hand and we left the meeting. There are some teachers who should not teach just as there are some counselors who should not counsel due to their beliefs about students and inmates' abilities to achieve. Some of these teachers and counselors' beliefs are destructive and damaging to students or inmates. There are too many inmates who are high school dropouts because of mean-spirited teachers and administrators. Many of our children are in pain as they grow into adults and they bring that pain with them. I've seen the pain in inmates when they reluctantly and embarrassingly tell me they cannot read. We must stop the cycle of miseducating our children and understand, when they are in our classrooms, they belong to us. It is our assignment as teachers to evoke, provoke, and inspire our children to exceed in their greatness to excel in their gifts. To parents I suggest you read Jawanza Kunjufu's book "Countering the Conspiracy to Destroy Black Boys". Dr. Kunjufu's will provide parents information that is key in preventing our children from becoming a "broken spirit."

BROKEN MEN AND WOMEN

In my seventeen years working with men and women who find themselves in prisons or halfway houses or those who are or have been addicted to alcohol, drugs, or have been molested, they all have one thing in common— pain. When we do not admit to ourselves what or who is causing us pain, we mask it, disguise it, or justify using or abusing alcohol, drugs, food, sex, shopping, gambling, etc. If we do not face our fears, we continue to blame others due to the lack of courage to confront our oppressors. This results in our continuing the abuse or being abused. Prior to my leaving Delaney Hall I had an in increase in the number of domestic violence cases among my caseload. I am sure other counselors experienced this as well. Many of our entertainers' resort to domestic violence as a means of solving their problems or dealing with their pain. As a counselor I give reference to some celebrities as examples to residents. A very popular artist, Lyfe Jennings, who is a genius in his own right, was arrested for domestic violence in October 2008. It was an altercation with the mother of his two children. Though he stated, "I did it, I know I got to be punished for it." "I just want the opportunity to apologize and that's it." He was charged with criminal trespass, discharging a firearm, his refusal to take a DUI test, in addition to two felony counts of attempting to elude an officer and possession of a firearm by a convicted felon. He pled guilty to all charges. In my lecture, this incident gave me the opportunity to discuss domestic violence and residents' relationships. We discussed the impact of Lyfe not being with his children and residents not being with their family because of their domestic violence charges. The discussion evolved to residents' admitting they wished they had it to do over again, they would not have put their hands on their wives, girlfriends, etc. Residents talked about their experiences seeing their parents fighting and stated that was what they saw growing up. In our discussions several topics came to surface: the need to control, rejection, when does no mean no, love does not hurt, when to walk away and the impact of their incarceration on their families. What would they have done differently to prevent them from going to prison? I support mental health therapy, anger management and employing counselors who have been trained to support individuals who come to these institutions who are confused, dangerous and in pain to get help.

Many of us have been in prisoned in our minds. I realized we do not have to have been in prison to know pain, confusion, helpless or scared. As a Black mother, I am afraid for my sons and male family members because of the systemic racism within the criminal injustice system. The Corona Virus once again exposed systemic racism in the medical, housing, and educational industries. All these behaviors contribute to men and women becoming broken spirits. Through my journey, I have learned the battle is in the mind. What you focus on expands, it becomes your reality. The process of investing in yourself is necessary to discover your purpose in life. You must put that work in to find you. That is why what you put in your mind is important. Who you surround yourself with is important? In the prison system, we talk to residents about who they surround themselves with, you know, people, places, and things. This is applicable to all of us.

When I realized, the battle, the war is in your mind, I realized speaking empowering words to yourself is key. Read inspirational books. My mind's environment is important to me.

You must live your truth and this process will bring you to your destiny. I am so grateful to have the opportunity to inspire.

Finally, everybody has a story. There are so many empowering stories. What inspires you to get the courage to be great? There is greatness in you. Live your purpose.

50 CENT & STEVE JOBS' LECTURE AT DELANEY HALL

Information packets supporting *50 Cent* and Steve Jobs Success Traits were distributed to inmates. I always pass out information packets so residents could take back to their rooms to read. After a lengthy engaging discussion on Steve Jobs and *50 Cent*, participants clearly understood the reasons why these two individuals were successful. Steve Jobs and his partner started Apple in Steve Job's parents' garage. *50 Cent* sold his CD's out of his car's trunk and used the principle of product sampling as he did with his drug-addicted clients. Steve Jobs was fired from his company and rehired after his success with Pixar and NeXT. *50* was shot nine times and survived. Studios wanted nothing to do with *50* because of the violence associated with him, but he continued to sell his CDs. Though Steve Jobs was fired from his company, he felt it was the best thing that happened to him. He became depressed however, and during this time, he created Pixar and NeXT. Subsequently, his company rehired him. Steve Jobs stated the experience confirmed to him the need to live his passion and do what he loved. He was determined to be successful. Eminem and Dr. Dre signed *50 Cent* on their label, Shady/Aftermath/Interscope Records. The release of Get Rich or Die Trying was phenomenal. Both men were determined, resourceful and risk-takers. Neither men set limits; they stood by their products, they followed their passion, did what they loved, and got paid for it. Fear was not part of their conversation. They surrounded themselves with successful individuals and embraced change. They also gave back to their communities. The passing of Steve Jobs was unfortunate, however, because of his genius and contribution in technology, his legacy will live forever. *50 Cent* is an example of great potential; you only need to stop making excuses. He was on the streets hustling, just like most inmates. I admire 50 Cent because he made the decision to change the trajectory of selling drugs in our community and destroying lives. Once 50 said no more he used his god given natural talents and as a result he is a successful entrepreneur. 50 Cent made millions from his Vitamin Water, he has grown his brands he continues to be a force to be reckoned with in the TV, movie, music industry. POWER, his successful mini-series on STARZ is remarkable. February 11, 2020 the beginning of the Covid 19 Pandemic For Life aired, another successful series this time local tv station, ABC by 50 Cent. However, this series specifically focuses on mass incarceration and the injustice of so many Black and Hispanics Americans who have been arrested and wrongfully convicted of crimes they did not commit. specifically, 50 Cent chose Isaac Wright, Jr. who was imprisoned for a crime he did not commit. While incarcerated Isaac Wright became an attorney and helped overturn wrongful convictions of twenty inmates, like The Innocence Project whose mission it is to bring reform to the system responsible for unjust imprisonment, with majority being Black men. In addition to overturning fellow inmates' cases, Isaac Wright proved his own innocence.

50 Cent is an impressive entrepreneur (Hustler) who is proving that when you live your TRUTH and change your attitude, you become extraordinary. There are some who will question why I selected 50 Cent to be included in Broken Spirits: Let it go so you can grow. 50 worked with the cards that were dealt to him in life. Rev. Robert Schuller says, "When life gives you lemons make lemonade". This is what 50 Cent did. I must interject here; we know the biggest drug dealers are the pharmaceutical companies who are destroying and killing the lives of Americans. I met 50 June 3, 2014, during his Animal Ambition Tour. I came to his tour because I wanted him to sign the 50th Law. Below is the inside of the book he autographed for me. There is a question I want to ask him on my TV Show, Tell a Vision that no one has ever asked him.

LEAVING THE KINTOCK GROUP
AND DELANEY HALL

The day I left the Kintock Group, I knew I would miss the ladies and guys. I resigned from Kintock in 2008, realizing it was time for me to do something more challenging. A coworker said to me that I would be excellent at Delaney Hall. They told me Delaney Hall was more structured and had larger groups and lectures. I applied to Delaney Hall. It was required that applicants present a lecture to residents and the residents would evaluate the presenter. I was hired. At first, I did not tell residents I was leaving; I didn't want Kintock residents to know where I was going. I informed the management. They told me they were sorry to see me go. They mentioned to me that for two years, I came in smiling every day. The Director called me in the office to congratulate me. He asked me if I let residents know. I said no. I didn't want them to know I was leaving. I mentioned that I have been giving them hints. He said, "Ms. Bey, you have to tell them because if you don't, they will think we fired you and that will be a problem for us. You have to let them it was your choice, Ms. Bey. We may have to send residents back to prison, they will be upset, we don't want a riot. We've never had a counselor who affected residents as you have, they love you; you have to tell them." I said okay; I did not want any of them to be sent back to prison. The next day I announced at the morning meeting that I accepted a new position at another facility, and my two weeks' notice was given to Kintock administration. I told the residents I would miss them. Some of them said "Ms. Bey, can we change your mind?" I said no. "When it's time to go, you leave. I will miss you, because you taught me so much, you have been so respectful to me, and I love you. Thank you."

The next day I came to work, I was not going to morning meeting because I was cleaning my office. One of the supervisors came to my office to tell me I had to go to the morning meeting. I told him I could not because I was cleaning my office. He said, "Ms. Bey, these guys stayed up all night to do something for you, you have to come."

"Okay," I said. I went to the hall. All residents—males and females—were in there. I was surprised. The cook said to me, "Ms. Bey I have been here for ten years, I have never seen this before." I said, "Really?" One brother beckoned me to the front; he was selected to present to me their gifts. He came forward with a teddy bear and basket, which I still have. He got on his knees and said "Ms. Bey, this is for you from us. We love you; we will miss you; we are happy for you. But can you change your mind and not go?" We all started laughing, and I said no. Everyone was there. The Director, the Director of Security, Human Resources, some of the cooks and counselors. Then he presented me with a plaque they made the night before with all their names on it. I felt like crying but didn't. I said thank you and that I loved them and would miss them. One of the residents said, "Ms. Bey I know you leaving but I put in a request slip for you, can I give it to you?" I said, yes. The ladies asked me to stop by to see them before I leave. I came by the ladies' area. They recited poems to me, gave me hugs, and thanked me for everything I had done for them even though some of them were not on my caseload. My last day, I treated my caseload to cake and ice cream, and we just talked. Before I left, the residents wrote this poem for me—reading it again made me cry again.

GOD's gift To Kintock
God has sent you from the heaven above,
=N= made you a Special Person that Everyone loves,
The day you walked into all our lives,
There were happiness =N= smiles that nobody could hide
Our lives became different in so many ways,

We became a big family through these months and days,
Our love for you became stronger than ever,
=N= we will always love u forever never,
God gave u a gift to touch us all,
=N= u will always be blessed most of all,
We enjoy your presence more than a little bit,
=N= nothing can ever change that because there was
nothing you lack,
Now that you are moving on to a better place,
We will always miss you because you can't be replaced,
The Kintock Group will never be the same,
But your memories here will always remain,
Congratulations on your new-found work,
You're a loving person who is down to earth,
May God Bless you =N= let nothing stress you,
You are the best =N= we'll never forget you,
Sincerely Yours .... The Kintock Residents

The following week I started orientation for Delaney Hall. During orientation, after hearing the challenges new employees would encounter working at Delaney Hall, several employees left. I began my job a week later at Delaney Hall. A strange thing happened: I was in my office, and a new resident knocked on the door. It was one of the residents on my caseload from Kintock. I was shocked. I asked what was he doing here. His response was "Ms. Bey, it changed when you left, you spoiled us."

"Wow. How?" I said.

"Because you did your job."

Here's the crazy thing: all my caseload was sent to Delaney Hall, along with other residents. I understood why the Director at Kintock asked me to tell them I was leaving.

I worked at Delaney Hall for six incredible years as a Senior Counselor and Program Counselor; this allowed me to grow and encourage residents to do the same. Soon I realized it was time to go and decided to inform residents I would be resigning to work in Mayor Ras Baraka's Reentry Program. Their response was similar to the response of the inmates at Kintock. I reminded them that when a person outgrows anything in life, you learn the lesson and move on to the next venture. The administration at Delaney Hall permitted me to develop my skills and be creative. I am very thankful to them. I was excited coming to work as I was when I worked at Kintock. Planning topics for groups and lectures was stimulating. Handling uncomfortable discussions in lectures or groups was challenging; however, it stirred the residents' thought processes—which was my goal. I needed them to stop complaining about where they were and stop blaming others for the choices they made. I encouraged them to use their time wisely rather than waste it by complaining, blaming, or making excuses. My lectures focused on their dreams, goals, passion, attitude, and solutions. I wanted them to concentrate on the greatness within them. They were encouraged to work on themselves by investing in themselves. I brought in books and lectured on the topic of those books. I copied book covers and pasted the covers on my wall. When residents sat at my desk, they would read while waiting for me. Many of the residents purchased the books that were on my wall. The residents and I started a group entitled Critical Thinking to Empower the Mind. Only those residents who were serious about changing their lives were admitted in the group. Residents knew what was discussed in the group stayed in the group. We had some powerful, spiritually moving sessions that transformed residents. After one of the sessions, a Caucasian brother said to me, "Ms. Bey, I paid so much money to those damn doctors, and I come to prison and you connected me to the source of my problem which was me. You helped me find me. I am free. I love you Ms. Bey."

"I love you too," I responded and smiled. Successful formally incarcerated men and women were brought in to speak to them. I wanted residents to witness men and women who sat where they were seated and because they did not make excuses, changed their attitudes—they were a testimony of success. Residents looked forward to seeing and hearing guests come in to speak to them.

Below is the original letter and the poem from my caseload and residents at Delaney Hall presented to me; I cried again (LOL)

Thank you for being a loving and caring person
Your concern and professionalism is without a doubt a
motivational factor to us
All I guess is what we're trying to say is
thank you for being you.
—Your Caseload
9/2014 poem from Delaney Hall Residents
Journeys are treasured, remembered forever
Moments come & go
Only time will show, the bonds built to last
Knowledge you've past, to help us to grow
Sincerely we say, Thank you, Ms. Bey

WHY I DID NOT WRITE UP RESIDENTS

Inside these programs, I noticed write-ups were utilized to punish rather than address behavior. I did not do write-ups. I addressed behavior. If they were given a second warning, I would give them a writing assignment; the third time, something they wanted was taken away such as a phone call or a visit. I remember an issue at Kintock. A resident was yelling and cursing at me in the lobby. He was upset because I denied his pass. I told him his behavior and threats did not change my mind. I would not approve his pass. I left the lobby to go to the lecture hall for a group.

I waited for the guys to be seated so I could begin. Before I could proceed, a brother said, "Ms. Bey, we saw what happened downstairs, are you going to write him up?" I said no, I would speak to him later. He said, "Ms. Bey we know how you feel about write-ups. But if you don't write him up, we're taking him to the bathroom." They just looked at me and they were not smiling, they were serious. I told them I would and started the lecture. After the lecture, I went back to my office and wrote the resident up, I gave it to the director to take to Parole which was on site. Parole called the resident to their office to inform him he was being transferred. The resident protested, saying he did not want to leave, and that he'd done nothing wrong. Per the director, the parole officer said, "Let me see who wrote you up." He looked at the write-up and said "You're outta here." "Why?" the resident said, and the parole officer responded, "Ms. Bey does not write-up residents, you had to have done something." He was transferred. That was the first time I realized what happens in the bathroom. It was my first and last write-up at Kintock.

WRITING LETTERS TO JUDGES FOR CLIENTS

I enjoyed writing letters for clients, particularly when clients are released. Letters to judges are important; it gave judges the opportunity to examine if inmates were following rules and regulations by attending required groups and lectures designated by the institution. I became known as the "get out of jail letter writer." However, I had stipulations. I did not simplify or embellish their charges, I was honest, nor did I lie when I wrote letters. Inmates had to have followed all the rules of the institution. A resident asked me to write a letter for him. I told him I would not because he would go to prison. Everyone in his room laughed. Why he said to me. Because you do not attend your groups, you got a bad attitude and your always mad and don't follow our rules and regulations. I'm not lying to the judge so you can go home. I will have to write the truth. So, that's why you will go to prison. So, I'm helping you out by not writing the letter. One resident was released from Delaney Hall because of my letter. However, he was upset the judge ordered him to attend anger management classes, which was one of my recommendations. I said to him, "but you were going to prison." I shook my head and said, "You do need anger management" and left the room. Another brother came to my office one afternoon and said, "Thank you, Ms. Bey." "Why?" I asked him. "Because of your letter, the judge released me, I won't be going to prison." "Wow." was my response, Then I said, "Let me see what I wrote." We both laughed. You see, I write so many letters, I forget what I wrote in the letters to the judge. I could have gone to my computer because I keep a copy of the letters but since he had it in his hand, I asked him to give it to me.

NEW JERSEY PERFORMING ARTS CENTER AND DELANEY HALL PROJECT

The Delaney Hall Writing Project with the New Jersey Performing Art Center was very successful. I met Baraka Sele, who was the VP at The New Jersey Performing Arts Center (NJPAC) in 2011. I invited her team to Delaney Hall to hear some of the artists at Delaney Hall. Behind the walls are very talented artists, musicians, poets, dancers, rappers, and singers. I wanted her to hear the residents perform. I informed the residents that Baraka Sele, Assistant Vice President of Programming Curator/Producer at NJPAC, and her team was coming in to hear the artists, and that we were considering partnering with New Jersey Performing Art Center to do an artist pilot project at Delaney Hall, funded by New Jersey Performing Art Center. Those residents who were interested in performing would have to sign up to perform. Ms. Gannon,

Clinical Director and Delaney Hall Administration was supportive. Baraka Sele and her team came to Delaney Hall. They were so spellbound and captivated by the residents' talent. Subsequently, the birth of NJPAC & Delaney Hall Writing Project took place. It was successful. Though brothers and sisters behind the wall are broken, they are brilliant and creative. One day I shared with residents my experience with a play I'd seen on Broadway. I was surprised that most residents had never seen a play. I brought in a casting company that presented a play about people who had been incarcerated, and one of the actors had been in prison for many years. The name of the play was **The Measure of a Man.** At the end of the play, there were no dry eyes. Some of the residents mentioned to me once they are released that they will take their families to see a play.

I conducted a lecture on "From Reel to Real" by Michael Bernard Beckwith. The topic was about our lives as a story; we are the directors of our stories, from make-believe to genuine individuals who have a purpose. Once the lecture was concluded, the inmates were given handouts on the topics. I indicated earlier as a counselor, the most critical aspect of my introduction to residents was the initial session with them. During these sessions, clients expressed to me the issues they were facing and why they were at Delaney Hall. Some were being transferred to a prison, and they were concerned whether they would make it or not. Assisting them in analyzing their circumstances were critical to their attitude. Getting to know their issues helped me develop groups and lectures for them. I brought in documentaries for them to watch, such as *The Secret, The Interrupters, Slavery by Another Name, Hidden Colors, Bloom, Where you are Planted* (by Joel Osteen), *The Answer is You* (Michael Bernard Beckwith), the last interview with Tupac, Les Brown, and Steve Harvey, and TD Jakes' motivation DVDs. There was always a discussion after the documentaries or discussions. Attitude and haters were still an exciting discussion as was changing their friends. As you can see, the administration at Delaney Hall did not limit my ability to reach the residents. Leaving Delaney Hall was not difficult because I knew I would see residents since I was leaving to work at Mayor Ras Baraka's Reentry Program. I worked with an exceptional staff who brought a wealth of knowledge to residents. Because of Councilwoman Bessie Walker, The Kintock Group, Delaney Hall, Essex County Correctional Facility, and Newark Reentry Services I learned the importance of attitude. Brothers and sisters allowed me to hone my skills, which allowed me to empower brothers and sisters behind the wall. I was not successful by myself. I reached out to several brothers and sisters who assisted or accompanied me to prison and halfway houses, and who assisted me in facilitating groups and lectures for residents at Kintock, Delaney Hall, Newark Reentry Services, and Essex County Correctional Facility, as well as other organizations, universities, colleges, and faith-based institutions. Councilwoman Bessie Walker, Ms. Kobt, Kintock), and Ms. Gannon, Delaney Hall) supported and believed in me. I resigned from Delaney Hall August 2014, armed with skills, knowledge, and information I planned to use at the Office of Reentry for the City of Newark under the leadership of Mayor Ras J. Baraka.

<u>CONCLUSION</u>

I wrote about the prison system and correlation to the failure of our school systems producing students for mass incarceration. I focused on preparation prior to their release from prison. Many of these inmates were damaged before they entered the prison system by society, they were "broken spirits." They were broken before they came to prison by their schools and homes. I cannot overemphasize the importance of having the right counselor or case manager assigned to residents, inmates so they can begin to heal. So, it is with our students. Students need supportive teachers to guide them in the choices they will make. Inspire, motivate and encourage them to prepare for their dreams in life. I have to tell this story. A young man came to my office one afternoon to inform me he was on my caseload. He had two tattoos on his face. Under one eye, "fuck" and the other eye "you." I informed him that before we proceed, I needed to know what was going on in his life at the time he put those words on his face. He said to me no one ever asked him that question. "I'm different." We smiled, then he told me his story. We do not know what our clients and students are going through. Currently I am reading Charlamagne tha God's latest book, *Shook One: Anxiety Playing Tricks on Me*. I thank Charlamagne for removing the embarrassment of seeking counseling—it does not insinuate we are weak; it implies we are courageous when we admit we need help.

There is no magic to this life. I know many brothers and sisters, including my White and Hispanic brothers and sisters, who are working with inmates in prison can understand what I am saying and have stories of their own. Staff can use this book to tell some of their stories that will help their inmates. Expose them to the EAGLE in them not the CHICKEN. Allow them to make the choice of who they want to be. However, owners and administrators of these public and private prisons and halfway houses must support changing inmates' stories to one of success by providing programs that will support them in their healing process before they leave prison because the change whether positive or negative begins in prison for better or worse. Teach inmates coping skills, how to handle life once they are released. Restorative justice is providing mental health strategies which is social justice. This is an opportunity for these institutions to become trailblazers in healing the human spirit rather than warehousing inmates, residents, or students to the land of nothingness. Inmates should be mandated to attend programs and activities not sleep in their cells or rooms. This is not preparing them for manhood or womanhood. Students should be expected to excel. I know those who are working in the system have the courage to bring out the greatness in their clients as I do and did. Inside the walls of our schools are our future, prepare and show them all the greatness they possess, instill in them a sense of pride. They will not become an inmate languishing behind the prison walls, they will see their challenges as positive and help them expand their possibilities Break the cycle of warehousing inmates, these brothers and sisters are geniuses, artists, masterminds behind the prison walls, cultivate their talents. If we become conscious in our responsibilities to revitalize inmates and students, we will restore their greatness which is what God intended us to accomplish. Owners of these private prisons and the cities they are house in have what my professor said to us "a window of opportunity". These prisons and halfway houses can be beneficial to their clients by creating an environment that will teach them skills to discover the greatness in them and make money. By focusing on their development, prisons or halfway houses will no longer warehouse inmates. My years of experience working with this population as well as my personal experience of having close family members who were in prison, in and out of prison, and who are still in prison, helped me write this book. My successes were based on materials I used to assist inmates and residents in their development in discovering themselves.

Those materials were books, CDs, and DVDs that I paid for, like so many of us do in this field and school systems. Guest speakers were brought in whose stories and experiences the residents related to. These speakers were former ex-offenders. I used books by these authors and others. Rev. T. D. Jakes, Pastor Joel Osteen, Iyanla Vanzant, Les Brown, *50 Cent*, Steve Jobs, Tupac Shakur, Steve Harvey, Michael Bernard Beckwith, the Hon. Elijah Muhammad, and Dr. Amos N. Wilson were influential when I planned my lectures. I wanted individuals who not only talked to the pain but showed how to grow through the pain, rise through pain. I tell inmates on a regular basis that once they are released back into society and face their issues, they will become a testimony of success for other inmates. Bringing in individuals they can relate to helped in their recovery process. It removed the "no excuses, blame game attitude"". I and those who work with this population have made significant differences in their lives—when we help others, we are helping ourselves. I thank Mrs. Reed, my teacher at Lafayette Jr. High School, in Elizabeth, NJ, a short white teacher who stayed after school with me when she noticed I was having difficulties, she instilled in me a thirst for learning. A teacher or counselor are powerful facilitators in the lives of students and inmates. The right teacher and counselor have an intense impact on students and inmates. For sure, broken individuals build broken families, broken school systems form broken prison systems. I say broken prison systems, because these systems are not about rehabilitation, it is about the money. Which is why I am so critical of school systems because I believe in many cases school systems prepare our children for the prison system. If this theory does not apply to you, let it fly. Michelle Alexander, author *The New Jim Crow: Mass Incarceration in The Age of Colorblindness*, was the Keynote Speaker spoke on prison reform at a Prison Conference at Bethany Baptist Church in Newark, NJ. I encourage those of you who are working on changing policies in the prison and educational system to read this book. Those who attended the Conference recognized the need to reform education and work within the prison system in order to help those who got caught up in the prison system. This Conference also discussed the need to change policies that seriously affect the lives of former ex-offenders and keeps them locked up in the system of failure. Because of these policies, many ex-offenders remain trapped in the system and as a result go back to what they know. Many of us who are fighting against these policies understand it makes our jobs difficult, but because of our commitment to the success of these brothers and sisters, our families and our communities, we continue to do what we do. We know many of our clients are "broken spirits." We assist them in their recovery. Thank you to brothers and sisters who are on the frontline fighting for justice and freedom. Below is a comment from Michelle Alexander's book The New Jim Crow, Mass Incarceration in the age of Colorblindness. I know I mentioned this earlier, but it requires a reminder that this book is a must read for anyone working in the prison system or who is concerned about social justice.

Michelle Alexander, states in her book "As of June 2001, there were nearly 20,000 more black men in the Illinois state prison system than enrolled in the state's public universities. In fact, there were more black men in the state's correctional facilities that year just on drug charges than the total number of black men enrolled in undergraduate degree programs in state universities".

It is my opinion based on my experiences that poor education, lack of opportunities, and lack of investments in our community's equal incarceration for our children, their parents, their friends, and our communities. People are getting paid to exploit and miseducate our children and subsequently incarcerate them. Restoring justice and investing in public education is imperative, it is necessary. Which is why we need individuals with the intention to restore justice and educate our children to be academically competitive. We also need politicians, executives in the prison system and public-school superintendents to work with us and the community to create a system that will transform individuals to be productive, responsible human beings. Once we understand this, I believe we will seriously hold our elected officials, superintendents, and educators accountable. Everybody is making money off our traumatic experiences in America. God's Plan is for us to live our purpose and become who we are destined to be. It is our stories that create our purpose so do not be embarrassed of your story; it is personal growth and transformative. I have included pictures, letters, and poems from residents as well as relative information regarding some of my experiences I mentioned in *Broken Spirit: Let It Go So You Can Grow.*

RE: RE: RE: RE: 1-7861320319 Broken Spirit: Let It Go So You Can Grow

---

From: Copyright Office cop-ad@loc.gov
Sent: Thursday, October 3, 2019 4:05:12 PM
To: maryambey18@msn.com maryambey18@msn.com
Subject: RE: RE: RE: RE: 1-7861320319 Broken Spirit: Let It Go So You Can Grow

Dear Maryam Bey,
Thank you for your response.

Your application has been approved and you should receive your certificate of registration in 3 weeks.

Sincerely,

Copyright Examiner

Literary Division
U.S. Copyright Office

Leaving The Kintock Group in 2008 was a sad day for because of the great staff and residents. My introductory to the criminal justice system via Kintock prepared me well. I loved working with the male and female inmates at Kintock.

An artist from Delaney drew this. So much talent behind the walls. That was the reason we partnered with Baraka Sele at The New Jersey Performing Arts Center. The Writing and Poetry Program for Delaney Hall is outlined below. I will never forget what Delaney Hall brothers and staff did for me, which is why I returned to provide services, information, trainings and job placement.

Kitab Rollins - Maryam Bey/Ellyn Gannon ... Poetry Program at Delaney Hall

From: Baraka Sele
To: ellenmgannon@yahoo.com; ellred230@aol.com; maryam bey
Date: 4/30/2010 7:59 PM
Subject: Maryam Bey/Ellyn Gannon ... Poetry Program at Delaney Hall
CC: Andrea Cummis; Kitab Rollins

TO: Ms. Maryam Bey
Ms. Ellyn Gannon
Delaney Hall
Newark, NJ

FROM: Ms. Baraka Sele
Assistant Vice President of Programming
Curator/Producer, NJPAC Alternate Routes
New Jersey Performing Arts Center
One Center Street
Newark, NJ 07102
973 642 8989 ext 5802
bsele@njpac.org

DATE: Friday, April 30, 2010

Maryam and Ellyn ... Kitab, Andrea and I cannot thank you enough for taking the time to meet with us yesterday at Delaney Hall. We are all so excited about your enthusiasm. We are grateful that you have eagerly and warmly embraced the idea of a pilot poetry program for the Delaney Hall residents.

1) We will need to develop an appropriate/interesting project title and description.

2) At your convenience, we will follow-up with a lunch meeting at NJPAC to further discuss how we might be able to accommodate both short and long-term residents.

3) The poetry program would include a series of writing workshops, as well as future poetry readings at Delaney Hall (possibly with poets who have performed at NJPAC)--and possible poetry readings at NJPAC with residents who successfully complete the program. Again, let me review a tentative program outline:

a) First Phase: introduce some of the poets who work with/perform at NJPAC to the Delaney Hall participants and have a poetry reading exchange.

b) Second Phase: poets who work with/perform at NJPAC would conduct/lead poetry writing workshops; perhaps one writing workshop per month for three months; at each session the correctional facility participants would be required to bring at least two written poems and they should be prepared to read the poems for comment/evaluation by the workshop leader and/or NJPAC staff.

c) Third Phase: after three months of workshop sessions, have a reading/performance at Delaney Hall for participants, counselors, staff (and some members of NJPAC staff).

4) We are also interested in being able to document/video-tape some of the sessions or performances in order to demonstrate/model the work that can be done through civic, community and cultural partnerships.

5) We are also interested in being able to develop a small book or publication regarding the project and some of the poetry that is created in the program.

We look forward to seeing you again soon ... Baraka Sele, Assistant Vice President of Programming, New Jersey Performing Arts Center

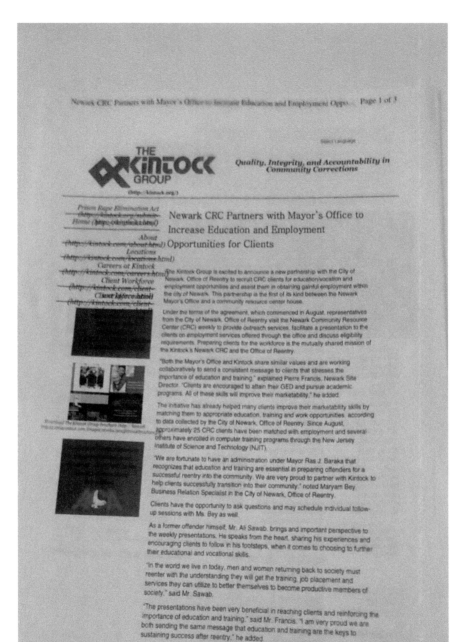

THE KINTOCK GROUP

(http://kintock.org/)

Quality, Integrity, and Accountability in Community Corrections

Newark CRC Partners with Mayor's Office to Increase Education and Employment Opportunities for Clients

The Kintock Group is excited to announce a new partnership with the City of Newark, Office of Reentry to recruit CRC clients for education/vocation and employment opportunities and assist them in obtaining gainful employment within the city of Newark. This partnership is the first of its kind between the Newark Mayor's Office and a community resource center house.

Under the terms of the agreement, which commenced in August, representatives from the City of Newark, Office of Reentry visit the Newark Community Resource Center (CRC) weekly to provide outreach services, facilitate a presentation to the clients on employment services offered through the office and discuss eligibility requirements. Preparing clients for the workforce is the mutually shared mission of the Kintock's Newark CRC and the Office of Reentry.

"Both the Mayor's Office and Kintock share similar values and are working collaboratively to send a consistent message to clients that stresses the importance of education and training," explained Pierre Francis, Newark Site Director. "Clients are encouraged to attain their GED and pursue academic programs. All of these skills will improve their marketability," he added.

The initiative has already helped many clients improve their marketability skills by matching them to appropriate education, training and work opportunities, according to data collected by the City of Newark, Office of Reentry. Since August, approximately 25 CRC clients have been matched with employment and several others have enrolled in computer training programs through the New Jersey Institute of Science and Technology (NJIT).

"We are fortunate to have an administration under Mayor Ras J. Baraka that recognizes that education and training are essential in preparing offenders for a successful reentry into the community. We are very proud to partner with Kintock to help clients successfully transition into their community," noted Maryam Bey, Business Relation Specialist in the City of Newark, Office of Reentry.

Clients have the opportunity to ask questions and may schedule individual follow-up sessions with Ms. Bey as well.

As a former offender himself, Mr. Ali Sawab, brings and important perspective to the weekly presentations. He speaks from the heart, sharing his experiences and encouraging clients to follow in his footsteps, when it comes to choosing to further their educational and vocational skills.

"In the world we live in today, men and women returning back to society must reenter with the understanding they will get the training, job placement and services they can utilize to better themselves to become productive members of society," said Mr. Sawab.

"The presentations have been very beneficial in reaching clients and reinforcing the importance of education and training," said Mr. Francis. "I am very proud we are both sending the same message that education and training are the keys to sustaining success after reentry," he added.

City Of **NEWARK** Mayor Ras J. Baraka

The Newark Municipal Council & NewarkWORKS

Addressing the needs of Newark's formerly incarcerated

Our mission is to service our Newark Re-Entry population, refer them to the appropriate providers and empower our Newark residents to obtain the education and job training skills in order to develop a career. Reentry services also provides preventative measures to deter Newark residents from becoming repeat offenders.

Services:

- Identification Assistance
- Legal Service Assistance
- Resume Preparation
- Job Readiness Training
- Vocational/ Career Training Referrals
- Clothing Assistance
- Job Placement Referrals / Educational Referrals
- Case Management
- License Restoration Referrals
- Housing Referrals

For More Information, Please Call or Email:

Maryam Bey, Coordinator
Reentry Services
990 Broad Street,
Newark, NJ 07102
973-733-8500
beym@ci.newark.nj.us

THE WHITE HOUSE

WASHINGTON

April 30, 2014

Ms. Maryam Bey
Newark, New Jersey

Dear Maryam:

Thank you for writing. As a country, we need to put every single child on the path to a great education and a good job. And I appreciate your thoughts on how we can help do that.

I have put forward some ideas of my own over the past year. I proposed a plan to expand access to early childhood education and make high-quality preschool available for every 4-year-old. I challenged my Administration to connect 99 percent of America's classrooms to high-speed Internet within 5 years. And we encouraged new partnerships to redesign our high schools so they equip every student with the tools to succeed in a high-tech economy.

These steps build on the progress we have already made. Since I took office, states have worked to develop smarter curricula and higher standards that prepare more students for college and career. And when Congress failed to fix No Child Left Behind, we partnered with states to give schools room to innovate while also raising standards and accountability.

These are the kind of bold investments we need to make in every part of our kids' education. But we also know that none of this will work unless we invest in our teachers, too. That means showing them support and respect worthy of the commitment they show every single day. And it means providing pathways to excellence that allow teachers to practice their craft with creativity and passion.

If we can do that—fund our schools, revamp our classrooms, uphold high standards, train the best educators, and stand behind them—we can do right by students all across our country. We can give them the shot at success they all deserve. And we can make sure America is a place where if you work hard in school, you can go as far as your talents will take you. That is what I will keep fighting for as long as I hold this Office.

Thank you, again, for writing. To learn more about my vision for America's education system, visit www.WhiteHouse.gov/Education.

Sincerely,

Barack Obama

RESOURCES

Those who are involved and support this system clearly understand that when someone is locked up and does not have resources—mainly money—the result will be to stay in prison until they are indicted, which can take up to six months. Connections allow residents to get resources. Most family members are hardworking and do not have funds to bail their loved ones out of jail. An effective attorney is necessary and not one who is going to convince clients to plead out if they are not guilty. Since inmates want to go home, they will accept a plea, not realizing that their pleas will give them a felony. Inmates fear they may lose their case and get more time, so they take the plea. It's a setup. An –eighteen-year-old man was arrested on gun charge and possession of CDS (controlled dangerous substance). He had no previous convictions. He had graduated from high school; he was on his way to becoming a career criminal. During my session with him, he mentioned he was told by his attorney that he should plead because if he goes to prison, he would be gone for a short period of time and when he returns, he would still be young. This attorney was not a public defender—the family was paying him. This client and his family trusted their attorney. They believed the attorney had their son's best interest in mind since they were paying him. Some attorneys work with the system to criminalize our children. I wrote a letter to this inmate's attorney. In the letter I described why it was important to prevent this young man from going to prison. I also gave recommendations that made sense. Once the attorney received my letter, he gave the recommendations to the judge and this young man was released. In the letter I made it very clear if he violated any recommendations, he would serve the full remainder of his time in prison.

Please visit these sites for resources, mentoring and research on criminal justice reform.

New Jersey Institute for Social Justice (njisj) located in Newark, N.J. Ryan P Haygood, President and CEO has been doing great work around social justice and reform. For more information and how you can join https://www.njisj.org/.

The Essex County Reentry Task Force Meetings are a valuable resource and great support system. I am a member. This is an organization comprising parole officers, probation officers, the Department of Labor, faith-based organizations, colleges, social workers, case managers, halfway houses, etc. These are individuals who care about the positive outcome of those incarcerated and returning home from prison. The members work on policies that affect returning citizens in housing, employment, mental health, family reunification, social justice, education, and training. If there is a Reentry Task Force in your city, become a member. The resources and contacts available to you to assist incarcerated and returning clients will be worth it.

Prodigal Sons and Daughters founded by Dennis Porter while he was in prison as a young boy. 1989 Dennis was released, he launched The Prodigals. Today, Prodigal Sons and Daughters has six locations. East Orange, New Jersey, Atlanta, Georgia, Newark, New Jersey and expanding to Africa. Their focus in mental health, housing, and employment.

RECOMMENDATIONS

The following recommendations will assist you with clients or students and provide them the trust they require to believe you have their best interest, as well as be genuine. However, you must be firm and respectful. These are some of the skills I learned as well as implemented over the years that served me well. Simply because I genuinely wanted to empower clients or students, so they would not return to prison or fail or drop out of school.

Listening Skills—Your initial consultation with your client and student will be the most important. This is the time you will acquire information that assists your client in their recovery and healing, or your student in their confidence to succeed. Your expectations will be valuable to a student. So, it is important they have your attention. Keenly listening enables you to know what questions to ask them.

Communication—An effective communicator can evoke greatness within their clients and students, wake up their dreams and purpose, encourage clients and students to soar in their minds. Their imagination is mind-blowing as well as unimaginable. They can visualize their dreams and begin to live their purpose. To accomplish this, they must have an inquisitive counselor or teacher.

Judgmental— Please do not be judgmental? So many times, inmates' (males and females) first sentence out of their mouths is, "I'm not a bad person." When I began working at the halfway house, I wondered why they were trying to convince me they were not a bad person; I didn't know them. After giving much thought to this statement, I realize they felt they were being judged or had been judged because they were locked up. I never judge, but I do not allow inmates to minimize their crime(s) I always remind them to look at the part they played in their incarceration. I let them know they were not innocent. Their response was always, "You're right, Ms. Bey." Most students admire their teachers, if they feel you are judging them negatively, it stunts their academic and emotional growth. Remember that when you are speaking to them. As a teacher, you are a powerful force, so be powerfully encouraging to them to discover their greatness within them. Therefore, communication skills are so essential. When I owned my school, our students rose to our teachers' expectations of them to be excellent.

Respect—This one is simple. Everyone wants to feel they matter, appreciated, valued, admired and special. So does your client or student. Put yourself in their shoes. How would it feel if you were devalued? The definition of respect is to be revered, honored, and appreciated.

Expectations—As a counselor or teacher, we must understand the importance of expectations, what a teacher thinks of a student does matter to them; they are living up to your expectations. Be careful as you have the power to destroy, thereby creating damaged goods, or you can inspire students to live the life they were destined to be. Your clients and students desire hope and optimism from you. Teachers are shaping and molding our future. Counselors are healing the pain, hurt, and brokenness of clients. Expectation means a lot.

No Excuses—When you allow clients to make excuses, they will not take responsibility for their action or behavior. As a counselor/case manager, you want clients to learn from their behavior and past mistakes, so they do not repeat it. Taking responsibility does not allow them to make excuses. Responsibility acknowledges they participated in their circumstances that they put the work in and paid for the chairs their butts are sitting, standing, or living in.

Attitude—As a counselor and case manager, attitude meant everything to me. My philosophy is a good attitude gets you in the door and a bad attitude throws you out. When I was an employment counselor, if residents had a bad attitude, I did not obtain employment for them until they changed their attitude and behavior. It was mandatory for the inmate to be released with a job; if not, inmates did not go home. Once they realized I was not changing my mind regarding their behavior, they changed their attitude because they wanted to go home. This taught me that if someone wanted it bad enough, whatever it was, they would change their attitude or behavior. It was based on how bad they wanted it. Some had not learned their lesson. They didn't want it bad enough at the time and were sent back to prison. Anything we want in life depends on how badly we want it.

Mindfulness or Consciousness—This is an important aspect of an inmate, resident, or returning citizen's success in society. I conducted a lecture on **pray** and **prey** and **telling** vs. **snitching**. I reminded the audience that I live in Newark. I used the analogy of us in Newark and urban areas praying for our communities to become safe, thriving, and prosperous. That we prayed for protection of our families. However, some of those same people were preying on us. I mentioned to the inmates or residents that some of them were predators in our community, robbing, raping and terrorizing our communities. As far as snitching was concerned, during my consultations with inmates, if they provided too much information about their crime, I would let them know, that's too much information and I am telling. Snitching is when two or more people are scheming to commit a crime and are then caught. In some instances, they become a betrayer, a squealer, an informant—that is a snitch. I would say I am not a snitch. So, if you give me too much information, I'm telling. Everyone would laugh.

My wall at Kintock, Delaney Hall, and Newark Sanitation Program was deliberately designed to extract responsibility, accountability, remorse and change in attitude so they made no excuses for their criminal activity. The pictures, book covers give them something to think about. When inmates or clients sat at my desk, while they waited for me, they had no choice but to read the contents on my wall. Inmates at Kintock or Delaney Hall would make comments like you must be smart, you ain't no joke, did you read all those books, or you demand respect. They were either inspired or would get quietly angry or in their conversation showed remorse. They would ask me questions about the contents of the book. I asked them to select any book and ask me any questions about the book. When I began my position as Career Advisor at Newark Works, I was asked by the director and Deputy Mayor to remove my book covers because it was not professional. I didn't listen. They did not have the experience I did with this population. My intention was to change behavior and criminal mindset. The contents on the wall gave them something to think about. The wall was also inspirational to clients and visitors who had not gone to jail or prison.

Mental Health Wellness—Most clients had survived some form of trauma. Most sisters—Black, Latina, White—I counseled were raped by a family member or someone they knew. They were still dealing with this pain. I clearly understood what they were articulating. Some brothers had father and mother issues, baby mama drama, racial profiling; some were raped or molested by family members or someone they knew. It was the first time they shared their pain and anger issues. Expressing their traumatic experiences was traumatizing for them. Releasing it in front of someone they trust was beneficial to their healing process. These experiences affected their success in school, which led to many students dropping out of school, beginning a criminal lifestyle, with the result of serving time in prison. So, it is imperative we have effective mental wellness in these systems that addresses mental health disabilities. Ask yourself what your intentions are as a counselor, case manager, or teacher. How do you want to help these individuals you are in charge of? Do you want to help them? If you are there to just collect a paycheck, you are not helping them. If you love what you do, you will find ways to assist them while they are in your care. You will think outside the box to reach them. You are influential. Your trust and confidentiality are important. The power is in your hand. Create a strategy that will empower and inspire clients and students to achieve their greatness they will be not be a Broken Spirit.

Understanding these systems are important. Education and mass incarceration are all about the money. I have no problem with that we must earn a living; however, when these systems are destroying people, specifically Black and Hispanic people, I have an issue with that. Investments should be made in public education, not charter schools. If charter schools are so good, why are they only in the urban districts? Charter schools have contributed to the destruction of public schools. I am providing a link on a recent article in The Washington Post by Valerie Strauss on charter schools https://www.washingtonpost.com/education/2019/12/09/r eport-federal-government-wasted-millions-dollars-charter-schools-that-never-opened/ In this article Diane Ravitch, Educator, Advocate for public education states "the Education Department has failed for years to properly monitor how its charter grant funding is spent". Diane Ravitch also stated Charter schools are financed by the public but privately operated". We must invest in public education not divest. Public education is mandated by law to accept ALL students. This link is informing the public President Trump and Education Secretary Betsy DeVos are seeking to slash $8.5 billion from Education Department https://www.mercurynews.com/2019/03/11/trump-seeks-to-slash-8-5-billion-from-education-department-budget-3/.

According to *The Washington Post*, dated March 11, 2019, President Trump seeks to slash $8.5 billion from the Education Department budget, by eliminating afterschool programs, teacher training, and grants for other school needs. That's not investing; that is incarcerating, decimating public education.

Prisons are profiting from 2.2 million people in them. The majority of prisoners are Black and Hispanic. The reason why I did not write up inmates were if they get these infractions, their sentence will be longer, or they may go to solitary. Corrections Corporations of America (CCA), a private prison, made a profit of $1.7 billion from incarcerating human beings. Practices require prisons to have 97% bed count to get funding. Michelle Alexander, author of The New Jim Crow Mass Incarceration in the Age of Colorblindness stated in her book that mass incarceration is the "New Jim Crow." President Bill Clinton's Crime Bill destroyed millions of Black families, and I voted for him twice. I didn't realize the impact it would have on Black people. According to http://www.bleausa.org/ dated November 28, 2019, US taxpayers spent almost $1 billion incarcerating innocent Black people. In many cases, it was because of wrongful convictions. Where is justice? White people commit crimes too. Now you can understand why Black and Hispanic parents worry about their family members. Former New York mayor and presidential candidate Michael Bloomberg recently apologized to Blacks and Hispanics for the "Stop and Frisk" policy that unlawfully profiled and arrested Blacks and Hispanics. You can read the article in this link https://time.com/5731264/bloomberg-apologizes-stop-and-frisk/ .

According to the Vera Institute of Justice, **incarceration costs an average of more than $31,000 per inmate,**

per year, nationwide. In some states, it's as much as $60,000. In New Jersey, the state I live in, the cost is $69,310. https://www.inquirer.com/philly/education/special-education-costs-new-jersey-budget-taxes-20180312.html

New Jersey Special Education cost varies depending on the categories. According to the above link Special Education costs are soaring and according to David Sciarra, Executive Director of the nonprofit Education Law Center. "The state sent districts $790 million that year in the other main form of special-education aid, although the formula required it to distribute $990 million". When you do your own investigation, you will discover that education and incarceration are big business. Attacking the most vulnerable. As many of us know it was once illegal to teach Black people to read. We were not slaves when we were kidnapped, we were made to be slaves. Many of you know that history shows us the Atlantic Slave Trade happened in 1619–1865; my question is, what happened before that? Then there was Jim Crow, 1877–1960s; Redlining, 1934–1968(this happens today); and mass incarceration, 1970s–present. Those of you who are counselors, case managers, and teachers think about the journey of Black people and ask the question, "How can I empower these broken spirits to bring hope, dreams, and fulfillment to their lives?" All the knowledge I have attained during my lifetime, the fact I was raped at fifteen, torn from my family, dropped out of high school, betrayals, horrific divorce, and more, I will not allow clients, residents, inmates, or students make excuses. This is called LIFE. I provide tools they will need to strengthen their path's journey. What I know for sure is all that I have been through in my life, I am grateful because my challenges allowed me to recognize my own inner and soul power that made me aware of my strength. My experiences helped me master my gifts that were given to me.

Inmates, residents and clients need emotional support, vocational training and mental health therapy these are three of their requirements if they are going to be successful in their release back into society. Students need a compassionate, understanding teacher who love children and want to see them grow and advance in a wholistic environment that is conducive to students' mental, physical, emotional, spiritual and creative development. This process with the support of their counselors and teachers, will give the opportunity to discover their POWER, take action towards their achievement and abundance in life. This is why my book is entitled "Broken Spirit." Let it go, so you can grow.

GUILTY AS CHARGED – DEREK CHAUVIN

There was no way I would revise Broken Spirit Let It Go without mentioning Derek Chauvin found guilty April 20, 2021, of all three charges for killing George Floyd. To add insult to injury, the family of a 16-year-old girl Ma'Khia Bryant was shot and killed Tuesday April 20th by a Columbus police officer as the nation was awaiting the guilty verdict of former Minnesota police officer Derek Chauvin. Though there was a guilty verdict the judge may not sentence Derek Chauvin to the maximum time but the minimum. Why do cops kill Black people? No consequences. If Black and White cops are receiving the same police training, why is it White cops kill Black people and Black cops do not kill White people? We will not tackle the issues of education, incarceration, the school to prison pipeline until we confront racism that allows them to incarcerate mainly Black people.

This is the first time a White cop has been found guilty of killing a Black man. Some may say this is justice, I say it is not enough considering the fact Black people continue to be killed by cops. There is a great need for police reform not abolishment but there must include consequences like loss of pension and sentenced to prison. This 400-year behavior of killing Black people is embedded in the criminal justice system. This is not equality. True reform in the police judicial system is warranted. Police know how to restrain themselves when White people commit crime, however, they chose to kill and abuse Black people. Let us remember a few casualties of many by the hands of those who are to protect and serve regardless of the color of their skin. Here are some names of documented killings of African Americans by cops. Of course, there are thousands more. Visit the site below to read names of those killed by cops.

Know their names: Black people killed by the police in the US *(aljazeera.com)*

2021 — Daunte Wright, 20 years, female cop, former union president.

2020 — George Floyd, 46 years old "knee on his neck"

2020 — Breonna Taylor, 26 years old

2015 — Freddie Gray

2014 — Tamir Rice, 12 years old

2014 — Eric Garner, 43 years old "I can't breathe".

1998 — James Byrd, 49 years old

1991 — Rodney King, 47 years old

1955 — Emmett Till, 14 years old Killed by a mob.

ABOUT THE AUTHOR

Maryam Bey, born Mary Lou Frazier, in Banks, Alabama, on April 6, 1951, was a "broken spirit." Her family were sharecroppers. They moved to New Jersey seeking work. At fifteen years old she was raped by her father and sent to Newark, NJ, to live with her mother's friend at sixteen years old. Maryam was devastated. Her young world was torn apart. Ripped from her brothers and friends through no fault of her own, she cried for ten years. She dropped out of high school in the twelfth grade due to pregnancy. Maryam eventually obtained her GED after passing the test with high scores at the Stevenson Institute of Technology in Hoboken, NJ. In 1974, with the assistance of her brothers and husband, she opened Creative Daycare Center that evolved into a school teaching student up to the fifth grade. It was licensed by the State of New Jersey. Maryam was twenty-four years old. In 1984, she closed Creative Garden when she was thirty-four years old. Maryam loved reading. She began purchasing books to seek answers regarding her personal issues. She attended workshops and conferences and purchased tapes. Maryam was investing in herself, finding herself, and healing herself. Books saved Maryam's life, which is why she refers to her books repeatedly in this book. Providing for four children and a grandchild was mentally demanding. Maryam prayed, cried, and sang. Singing was Maryam's passion. Before she was raped, she aspired to be a singer and had joined a singing group. Her group performed at the Amateur Hour at the famous Apollo Theater in Harlem, New York City, and the group came in second place. Maryam won several singing contests thereafter. Once Maryam closed her school, she became involved in politics. She ran for Newark school board member six times before she was elected in 2001. She was elected Board President by her board colleagues. Maryam ran for Councilwoman twice. The Kintock Group, Delaney Hall, Office of Reentry for the City of Newark, Essex County Correctional Facility, and New Jersey Reentry Corporation—all contributed to her success in reentry. She is the CEO of Tell a Vision, LLC—a local cable program TV show and public speaking firm. Maryam did not know that through all her personal trials, challenges, and sufferings, one day she would apply those experiences and skills to help others understand their purpose. Maryam made no excuses, and she does not accept excuses from her clients. She earned two degrees from Saint Peter's University in Jersey City, New Jersey, in Education and Public Policy. In 1994, Maryam purchased her first home in the west ward of Newark. This was accomplished as Maryam worked full-time and part-time jobs, supported a family, while going through a painful divorce. You can contact Maryam and her team for lectures, staff development trainings, and speaking engagements.

Contact information: www.maryambey.com, www.tellavisiontav.com, maryambey18@msn.com, and 973.699.8978.

Maryam added Let It Go So You Can Grow to Broken Spirit, once she recognized through her counselling inmates who held onto their pain and traumas rather than letting it go remained stuck in their pain. Working with and counselling majority Black and Hispanic inmates gave Maryam the opportunity to help them realize their greatness and discover their purpose. Maryam's intentions are to discuss mass incarceration, the impact in the educated system and society and how we change the paradigm. There are individuals of all races who realize we must fix this injustice. Case managers, counsellors, teachers are critical to the academic, vocational advancement of inmates and students, which is why criminalizing their behaviour is not the answer.

"BROKEN SPIRIT: Let It Go So You Can Grow" is a compilation of my years working with brothers and sisters behind the walls and assisting them to begin their entrance back into society. The re-entry process begins while individuals are incarcerated. Therefore, counselors and case managers are critical to inmates' successful re-entry. I began my career at The Kintock Group in 2006 as an Employment Counselor and went on to Delaney Hall as a Program Counselor in 2008, Office of Newark Reentry in 2014, and Essex County Correctional Facility in 2016 as a job readiness trainer. I was stunned to discover that most inmates were high school dropouts which led me to recognize the correlation between education and mass incarceration or the school prison pipeline.

I had no idea that the books I used for my personal development and transformation would years later be utilized to benefit incarcerated brothers and sisters as a way to manifest the greatness within them. "BROKEN SPIRIT: Let It Go So You Can Grow" is dedicated to counselors and case managers who work with inmates and to public school teachers who educate students. Counselors and teachers have the responsibility of training, inspiring, and instructing individuals to live their dreams and purpose. University and college students who are considering a career as attorneys will find this information uplifting. I encourage all re-entry specialists to use the stories in "BROKEN SPIRIT" to empower inmates, students, and staff. These stories will assist counselors and teachers in their training, groups, or lectures. We must encourage inmates and students to take full responsibility for their actions so that they can manifest their inner greatness. There is no room for excuses and attitude is everything. So, to all "broken spirits" whatever is not serving you, "let it go so you can grow".